Growth Theory

Growth Theory

AN EXPOSITION

——

R. M. SOLOW

——

The Radcliffe Lectures
Delivered in the University of Warwick
1969

——

1970
OXFORD UNIVERSITY PRESS
New York and Oxford

Preface

I HAVE taught the theory of economic growth to successive classes of graduate students at M.I.T. for more years than I like to remember. I was, therefore, doubly grateful to Professor J. R. Sargent and the University of Warwick, not only for the honor of an invitation to deliver the first series of Radcliffe Lectures, but also for their exquisite taste in suggesting that they would like to hear an exposition of growth theory. This little book is a modified version of the six lectures that I gave at Warwick in December 1968 and January 1969. I have added some mathematical material that should help the interested reader to understand the structure of the theory but would have been inappropriate in a short series of lectures. Much of the flavor of spoken lectures remains in the text, but I hope that is not a bad thing in what is intended as an exposition.

I have tried to present the theory of economic growth as a theory that tells something—though obviously not everything—about the laws of motion of some kinds of economic systems. Where important issues have been neglected— those connected with effective demand, for instance—I have neglected them fairly and squarely, to alert the reader. When I lecture at leisure on this subject, I spend much more time on matters of analytical technique than I do here. What I have tried to do in six short chapters is to give some feeling for the scope of the aggregative theory of growth, some notion of the technical details, without pretence of completeness, and some idea of the directions in which future research is likely to go.

I owe a debt of thanks to Professor Sargent and the other economists at the University of Warwick for the friendly reception they gave me during my visits. The staff of the Clarendon Press have been as kind and forebearing as one could wish. These lectures were delivered and revised during my year as George Eastman Visiting Professor at the

University of Oxford. It is a pleasure to send thanks to those connected with the Eastman Professorship, to Oxford's economists, and above all to the Master and Fellows of Balliol College for their warm welcome. I want also to make acknowledgement to the various friends from whose work I have cribbed, and to generations of students at M.I.T. who have imposed their own standards on my teaching, and many of whom are now doing the hard work of pushing forward the theory of economic growth.

Massachusetts Institute of Technology   R.M.S.
December 1969

Contents

Growth Theory

1

Characteristics of Steady States

MY object in this book is to survey the macroeconomic theory of growth as it has developed since events and Harrod and Domar revived our interest in compound interest. It is a theory with a fairly simple skeleton, although it is capable of a quite surprising amount of elaboration. My summary will have to be limited to the main bones in the skeleton. To review all the possible details, wrinkles, and variations on the basic outline would take much too long; the famous Hahn–Matthews survey occupied more than 100 pages of the *Economic Journal* and had a bibliography of nearly 250 items, and that was 4 years ago. Quite a lot more has been done since then. Besides, a book on this scale is not the appropriate medium for that kind of survey. Textbooks are on the way.

What I want to do is to discuss questions like the following. What features of economic life is the theory of growth supposed to describe or explain? How does it go about describing them and how well does it succeed? Finally, and here I will have to be very selective, what does the theory suggest about managing the sort of economy it succeeds in describing?

Please keep in mind that we are dealing with a drastically simplified story, a 'parable', which my dictionary defines as 'a fictitious narrative or allegory (usually something that might naturally occur) by which moral or spiritual relations are typically set forth'. If moral or spiritual relations, why not economic? You ask of a parable not if it is literally true, but if it is well told. Even a well-told parable has limited applicability. There are always tacit or explicit assumptions underlying a simplified story. They may not matter for the point the parable is trying to make; that is what makes parables possible. When they do matter, the parable may mislead. There are always aspects of economic life that are left out of any simplified model. There will therefore be problems on which it throws no light at all; worse yet, there may be problems on which it appears to throw light, but on which it actually propagates error. It is sometimes difficult to tell one kind of situation from the other. All anyone can do is to try honestly to limit the use of a parable to the domain in which it is not actually misleading, and that is not always knowable in advance.

What are the broad facts about the growth of advanced industrial economies that a well-told model must be capable of reproducing? In 1958 Nicholas Kaldor summed them up in the form of six 'stylized facts'. There is no doubt that they are stylized, though it is possible to question whether they are facts. Facts or not, they are what most of the theory of economic growth actually explains, so they are worth stating.

(1) Real output per man (or per man-hour) grows at a more or less constant rate over fairly long periods of time. There are short-run fluctuations, of course, and even changes from one quarter-century to another. But at least there is no clear systematic tendency for the rate of increase of productivity in this sense to accelerate or to slow down. If, in addition, labour input (population modified by variations in the participation rate and annual hours worked) grows at a steady rate, so will aggregate output. Since output is the product of labour input and output per unit of labour input, the rate of growth of output will be the sum of the rates of growth of labour input and of productivity.

(2) The stock of real capital, crudely measured, grows at a more or less constant rate exceeding the rate of growth of labour input. So capital per man can also be said to grow at a more or less steady rate over fairly long periods of time, subject to qualifications about short-run irregularities and occasional breaks in trend.

(3) Moreover, the rates of growth of real output and the stock of capital goods tend to be about the same, so that the ratio of capital to output shows no systematic trend. This is

a rather more controversial reading of the facts, for two sets of reasons. First, there are problems of definition and measurement: (a) the ratio of capital to output is very volatile in any fluctuating economy, because the stock of capital is necessarily a sluggish time series, while output is capable of making wide swings in short intervals; (b) we ought really to be interested in the flow of services from the stock of capital, while we actually have measurements of the stock of capital, and the two can diverge not only through changes in the margin of idle capacity (which is really the point made under (a)), but also through variations in shift work, 'down time', running speed, and the like; (c) although I shall be reasoning in terms of a model with only one commodity, so that relative prices do not enter, our data do not come from such a world. If we think of capital as a factor of production, it is presumably the 'real' capital stock that matters, but if we think of it as a store of wealth, it is presumably the value of the capital stock in terms of consumer goods that matters, and both capital/output ratios can be constant only if the price of capital goods relative to consumer goods is constant, as it has not in fact always been. Secondly, the data are far from clear about the constancy of the capital/output ratio, however the measurement problems are resolved.

(4) The rate of profit on capital has a horizontal trend, apart from occasional violent changes associated with sharp variations in effective demand.

The two remaining 'stylized facts' are of a different kind, and will concern me less, because they relate more to com parisons between different economies than to the course of events within any one economy.

(5) The rate of growth of output per man can vary quite a lot from one country to another.

(6) Economies with a high share of profits in income tend to have a high ratio of investment to output.

The third and fourth 'stylized facts' already imply that the share of profits in total income will be constant, or at least trendless, in the process of economic growth. If the rate of profit and the capital/output ratio are both constant, then their product, which is the share of profits in total output or income, must also be constant. The second and third 'stylized facts' imply similarly that the ratio of (net) investment to output is constant. To say that the stock of capital grows at a steady rate is to say that the ratio of net investment to the stock of capital is more or less constant. Together with the constancy of the capital/output ratio, that requires the ratio of net investment to output to be constant.

An economy growing according to the first three (or perhaps four) of these rules is said nowadays to be in a 'steady state'. Its output, employment, and capital stock grow exponentially, and its capital/output ratio is constant. It is more convenient, usually, to define a steady state by the requirement that output and employment be growing at some constant proportional rates and that net saving and investment be a constant fraction of output. For then net investment must be growing at the same proportional rate as output, and so must the stock of capital, which is the sum of past net investments. The capital/output ratio will therefore be constant. The advantage of this more compact way of putting it is that we sometimes feel more confident that we know what we mean by output and saving than that we know what we mean by the stock of capital. Even if it is illegitimate and pointless to add last year's investment to this year's, we may be able to use this alternative definition of a steady state. (This is not to assume that the saving rate is an independent constant. It may depend on anything, so long as those things are constant or offsetting in a steady state. The saving rate may thus be different in different steady states, if there is more than one possible.)

Most of the modern theory of economic growth is devoted to analyzing the properties of steady states and to finding out whether an economy not initially in a steady state will evolve into one if it proceeds under specified rules of the game. It is worth looking at some figures to see if the steady-state picture does actually give a fair shorthand summary of the facts of life in advanced industrial economies. The reason it is worth doing is not simply to say yes or no, to accept or reject the steady state as a theoretical construct. No such simple description will ever fit the facts very well. If it bears no relation at all to what one sees, then obviously one will be suspicious of any theory that clings to the steady state. It is more likely, however, that the data will be neither perfectly consistent nor utterly inconsistent with the 'stylized facts'. One wants, then, some indication of the importance of having a flexible theory that is capable of explaining approximate steady states but has at the same time a reasonable escape hatch, a way of accounting for systematic divergence from the steady state. Of course one must not go too far; a theory capable of explaining anything that might possibly be observed is hardly a theory at all.

One useful source of information is Denison's book *Why Growth Rates Differ*, which provides comparable information for the United States, the United Kingdom, Belgium, Denmark, France, Germany, Italy, the Netherlands, and Norway. Unfortunately, the time period covered runs only from 1950 to 1962, so we can not hope to learn anything about the relative steadiness of rates of growth. But some of the other stylized facts can be checked.

It appears, for example, that the capital/output ratio has a clear trend in most of the nine countries. The Netherlands is just about the only one that behaves according to Kaldor's rules in this respect; its real national income grew faster than its gross stock of business fixed capital, but slower than its net stock of capital. In some of the other countries, however, the difference between the rates of growth of output and capital is slight (for example, 3·3 and 3·7 per cent a year in the U.S., 3·2 and 2·9 per cent a year in Belgium). Moreover, the direction of the trend in the capital/output ratio was not the same in all countries. It was rising in the U.S., Denmark, Norway, and the U.K., falling in Belgium, France, Germany, and Italy.

Similar results emerge from some unpublished data of Harold Barger's, which differ in definition and coverage from Denison's. (Barger's output excludes the rent on houses, and his capital stock—like Denison's—excludes the houses themselves; Barger includes government capital.) According to these figures, the capital/output ratio rose between 1950 and 1964 in the U.K. (very slightly), Germany, Denmark, Norway, and Sweden. It fell in France, Italy, the Netherlands, and the U.S. In Barger's as in Denison's figures, substantially rising and falling capital/output ratios occur with about equal frequency; but notice that the United States and Germany change sides in the two bodies of data.

In my view, the constancy of the capital/output ratio does not come off too badly. One clearly wants to be prepared for the capital/output ratio to move in one direction or the other in a fairly sustained way. But there is no presumption about the direction, so in that sense, at least, theory ought to be neutral about the relation between the rates of growth of capital and output. The unstylized facts will hardly justify anything more than an agnostic conclusion.

Denison provides no direct information on the rate of profit on capital. He does give some figures on the share of profits in total income, and those, together with what we know about the capital/output ratio, will permit some inferences.

In seven out of Denison's nine countries, the return to plant and equipment as a proportion of national income was lower in 1960–2 than in 1955–9 and lower in 1955–9 than in 1950–4. The only exceptions were Denmark and Germany. Even in those countries the share of plant and equipment was lower at the end of the period than at the beginning, but only by a negligibly small margin; and in the case of Germany the share of plant and equipment actually rose and then fell. It would be clearly premature to substitute an empirical law of the falling share of profits for what many people used to think of as a law of constant relative shares. But this tendency for the earnings of plant and equipment to fall relative to national income is probably not a mere statistical accident. It seems to have occurred in too many places for that; and in addition, longer time series for the United States and the United Kingdom suggest that the tendency may go back to the first quarter of the century, and perhaps further.

Now the rate of profit on capital is algebraically equal to the share of profits in income divided by the ratio of capital to income (or output). (There are all sorts of difficulties about the definition of the rate of return on capital and the measurement of the value of capital; one ought to be wary of attaching precise meaning to small statistical differences.) Wherever the share of profits has been falling and the capital/output ratio rising or stationary, the rate of profit on capital must have been falling. That covers the Netherlands, the U.S., Denmark, Norway, and the U.K. among the countries studied by Denison. (It is likely that the falling rate of profit recorded for the U.S. is an illusion; Denison's series end too early to pick up an improvement in profits after 1962.) In the remaining four countries, it would take a finer examination to tell what has happened to the rate of profit; in some of them, the best guess would be that it has shown no trend in either direction.

Longer time series for the U.S. and the U.K. confirm this general picture. The key ratios are not stable, as the literal steady-state picture would demand, but they move slowly and sometimes change direction. In the U.S. the capital/output ratio was falling from 1919 to World War II, and constant or rising slightly afterwards. The share of profits in total income may have been falling slightly for a long time, despite a sharp increase just after the war; but the rate of profit on capital was probably rising during the period when the capital/output ratio was falling. The depression put an end to that of course.

For the U.K., the figures of Matthews and Feinstein suggest that the capital/output ratio was falling from 1856 to 1899, rising from 1899 to 1913, falling slightly from 1924 to 1937, and essentially stable after the war. The share of profits in income has been generally falling during this century, but not much has happened to the rate of profit.

My general conclusion is that the steady state is not a bad place for the theory of growth to start, but may be a dangerous place for it to end. In fact, as you will see, much of the analysis we have is about steady states. The theory contains some leads about mechanisms that could cause systematically different behaviour. They have not been followed up very much, partly for mathematical reasons, partly because those mechanisms depend on factors that are intrinsically difficult to measure, perhaps especially at the macrolevel, but perhaps anyway.

THE HARROD–DOMAR CONSISTENCY CONDITIONS

Harrod and Domar, in different ways, posed a basic question: under what circumstances is an economy capable of steady-state growth? That is by no means the only question they discussed, but it is the one that has given rise to most of the subsequent discussion. Notice that I say 'an' economy, because much of the emphasis falls on matters that depend hardly at all on the institutional framework of the economy. The matters that have to do more specifically with the behaviour of a capitalist economy are more obscure, and lead to difficult questions that have not yet been fully answered.

The best way to get at this basic question is to invent the simplest possible model economy and make some very special assumptions about its characteristics. We can then see where they lead. The assumptions, or some of them, will be seen to flow directly from the central notion of a steady state.

The model economy produces only one composite commodity, which it can either consume currently or accumulate as a stock of capital. It has a supply of homogeneous labour which is used, together with the stock of capital available from past accumulation, as an input to current production. We are obviously in the world of parable. We make three specific assumptions about this model economy.

(1) The population and labour force grow at a constant proportional rate that is independent of other economic forces. I shall call this rate n.

(2) Net saving and investment are a fixed fraction of net output at any instant of time. I shall call this fraction s. In the context of a capitalist economy, the saving rate is just a behaviour parameter; it is what it is. Later on I will con-

sider some alternative ways of describing saving behaviour. In the context of a planned economy, the saving rate is just a policy parameter; for present purposes its value has been chosen and fixed, and we are interested in the consequences of that choice.

(3) The technology of the model economy is fully described by two constant coefficients. One is the labour requirement per unit of output, and the other is the capital requirement per unit of output, which I shall call v. They are fixed numbers, both in the sense that they can not be varied at any instant of time, and in the sense that they do not change in the course of time. The technology of the economy has fixed coefficients; and no technological change is taking place. We shall later have to reconsider both assumptions. The capital/output ratio is supposed already to include an allowance for normal excess capacity.

The question is now: are these assumptions compatible or consistent as a description of a growing economy? Is the model economy capable of generating steady-state growth? The characteristic answer given by Harrod and Domar was that they are compatible if and only if $s = vn$, the saving rate is the product of the capital/output ratio and the rate of growth of the labour force. There are various ways to make this famous point; my way is not the easiest, but it will help later on. The number nv is the proportion of investment to output just necessary to keep the stock of capital growing at the same rate as the supply of labour. If the labour force grows at 1 per cent a year, then investment must be 1 per cent of the capital stock if capital per man is to be constant. That means that investment per unit of output must be 1 per cent of the capital/output ratio. The Harrod–Domar consistency condition says that the savings rate must be just equal to that required ratio of investment to output for a steady state to be possible.

Suppose it is not. Suppose the saving rate exceeds vn. Then if the unemployment rate is somehow held constant, so that employment grows as fast as the labour force, each year's saving and investment must be more than enough to provide capital for the annual increment to employment, so the economy must be adding to its excess capacity every year, over and above the normal excess capacity already included in v. Alternatively, if the economy insists on using all the capacity it creates by investment, it can do so only by increasing employment faster than the labour force grows, so eventually the economy will run out of labour, and revert to the first state of affairs. In other words, if s exceeds vn, the saving or investment effort is so large that, if all available capacity is manned, the supply of labour is inadequate to man it in the required fixed proportions; or, if only that capacity is manned for which labour can be found, there must be perpetual addition to excess capacity.

If s is less than vn, the proportion of investment to output is less than that required to keep the capital stock growing as fast as the labour force. If the economy tries to keep the unemployment rate constant, it will eventually run out of capacity; if it tries to keep the margin of excess capacity fixed, employment will rise more slowly than the labour force and the unemployment rate will rise towards 100 per cent. The economy saves and invests so little that it fails to create enough new capital to provide the possibility of employment for the annual increment to the labour force. Either there will be more and more unemployment, or the economy must be using up a margin of excess capacity, which will eventually disappear. Of course, some combination of both outcomes is possible.

What will actually happen in such an economy depends on aspects of its behaviour that have not been specified. The problem would arise even in a planned economy that was faced with given n and v and happened to choose an s different from the product of v and n. It is much easier to guess how a planned or even crudely managed economy would react, than to work out all the implications for a capitalist economy.

In any case, the possibility of a steady state, a state of affairs with constant saving rate, capital/output ratio, and **rate** of growth of labour force, depends on the satisfaction of the consistency condition $s = vn$. Then and only then will the flow of additions to capacity just match the annual increment to the labour force, as of a constant ratio of capital to output.

In this, which I will call, with some injustice, the Harrod–Domar version of the parable, the numbers s, v, and n are independently given facts of nature. The rate of growth of the labour supply depends primarily on those demographic factors that influence birth rates and death rates, and on those sociological factors that in the long run influence the choice between participation in the labour force and non-participation. The capital/output ratio is intended to be a technological fact only slightly, if at all, capable of variation in response to economic forces. The saving rate is supposed to describe still another set of facts, attitudes towards consumption and the ownership of wealth (though Harrod saw perfectly well that, if there is a life-cycle pattern to saving, the overall saving rate will vary with the age-distribution of the population, and therefore with the rate of population growth—an idea much in favour again).

This poses a problem. If s, v, and n are independent constants, then there is no reason at all why it should happen that $s = vn$, except by the merest fluke. But then capitalist economies should be incapable of steady-state growth, except perhaps if it is accompanied by a perpetual build-up of excess capacity (maybe with a tight labour market) or by a steadily worsening unemployment rate (maybe with extraordinarily high utilization of capacity). Steady-state growth, constant saving rate, constant capital/output ratio, accompanied by only limited fluctuations of the unemployment rate and the capacity-utilization rate, should be a rare state of affairs, except in planned economies. Yet Kaldor's stylized description of the growing economy, reinforced by a casual glance at the facts, suggests just the opposite. If it is too much to say that steady-state growth is the normal state of affairs in advanced capitalist economies, it is not too much to say that divergences from steady-state growth appear to be fairly small, casual, and hardly self-accentuating. You would not react to the sight of an economy in steady-state growth as you would react to the sight of a pendulum balanced upside-down, or a vacuum sitting in plain daylight while Nature abhors it.

VARIABLE POPULATION GROWTH AND SAVING RATE

With this general kind of model, there is only one way out of the box. At least one and perhaps more of the three numbers s, v, and n must be, not a given constant, but a variable capable of taking on a sufficiently wide range of values. That would be enough to establish the bare possibility of steady-state growth. Something more is needed, however, to account for the prevalence of steady or near-steady growth in actual economies. What is needed, ideally, is some plausible mechanism to drive the one or more variables among s, v, and n into a configuration in which the Harrod–Domar consistency condition is satisfied. One could settle for something less, a route by which the appropriate changes in s, v, and n could come about under favourable and not-too-implausible circumstances.

Which among the three key parameters is the likeliest candidate for the role of the variable? It is interesting that the classical economists would presumably have agreed first on the one of the three that modern theorists tend to take as the only constant—the rate of population growth. I presume that this difference in theoretical strategy reflects a genuine historical change in the sensitivity of population growth to economic factors. It is not hard to believe that the balance of births and deaths is more open to influence from economic events at low standards of living than at higher.

Nor is it hard to tell a consistent story in which the rate of population growth is driven to the value s/v, so the Harrod–Domar condition is eventually satisfied, though the story may not reflect modern economic conditions very well. One has to assume that investment proceeds in such a way as to keep the margin of excess capacity roughly constant. Then if s is less than vn, so that the economy does not invest enough to employ its labour force, the result will be an increasing unemployment rate. So far the story is just as before. But if rising unemployment, probably accompanied by falling wages, eventually depresses the rate of population growth, the gap between s and vn will be narrowed, and the process can continue until the gap is closed. In the opposite case, when these rules of the game produce more investment than is required to employ the growing labour force, but all capacity gets into productive use, the labour market will become very tight, real wages will presumably rise, and the rate of population growth will respond by increasing until the Harrod–Domar condition is fulfilled. I hardly need to add that this story requires outlandish assumptions to make investment behaviour more passive than one would expect it to be in an industrial capitalist economy.

Even under the best of circumstances, however, no one would depend on this Malthusian adjustment process to account for the ability of modern economies to maintain a constant saving rate and steady growth for 20 years at a time without catastrophe. It has, however, been suggested that systematic changes in the saving rate can and do provide a vehicle for semi-automatic satisfaction of the Harrod–Domar consistency condition. There is, of course, no excuse for treating the saving ratio as a constant—except perhaps that it does not seem to change much in the absence of violent fluctuations of effective demand. Alternative theories of the endogenous determination of the saving rate have been worked out—life-cycle theories, permanent-income theories, utility-maximization theories—and some of them have been found to give a satisfactory explanation of data. I will come back to them in another context.

The endogenous theory of saving that is most often invoked to help account for steady states is the simple one that different but constant fractions of wage income and non-wage income are saved, that a larger fraction of non-wage income (or profits, for short) is saved, and that therefore the aggregate saving ratio for the whole economy is higher the higher is the share of profits in total income. In fact, the aggregate saving ratio is a weighted average of the two given saving ratios, with weights equal to the respective distributive shares. The aggregate saving rate can, in principle, have any value between the saving rate from wages and the saving rate from profits. If vn falls anywhere inside that range, then the Harrod–Domar condition can be satisfied, and steady-state growth is at least possible. To bring it about, the distribution of income must be just right, and a question arises about the mechanism that moves the distribution of income.

The mechanism that seems to be required goes something like this. The economy tends to operate with a constant unemployment rate. Suppose that the distribution of income between wages and profits is such as to generate a saving ratio larger than vn. I reasoned earlier that if the unemployment rate is indeed steady, then initially the margin of excess capacity must be getting larger. With unemployment steady and capacity utilization falling, one would expect profit margins to weaken relative to wage costs per unit of output. But that is the same thing as a shift in the proportional distribution of income in favour of wages against profits. Because a smaller fraction of wages is saved, the aggregate saving ratio falls and comes closer to vn. This process will go on until steady growth is established. The unemployment rate and capacity-utilization rate will have to be compatible with an unchanging distribution of income. If, initially, the saving rate were less than vn the same process would work in reverse. A sluggish unemployment rate would lead to increasing pressure on capacity, widening margins, a shift of income distribution in favour of profits, and a rise in the aggregate saving rate, until the Harrod–Domar condition were satisfied.

From one point of view, it is immaterial in this story whether it is the capacity-utilization rate or the unemployment rate that moves. For instance, in the case where s is bigger than vn, a steady utilization rate would have to mean a falling unemployment rate and therefore a distributional shift away from profits, and a fall in the saving rate. But the story is obviously better the way I told it the first time. The margin of excess capacity is in fact more volatile than the unemployment rate, in the American economy at any rate. Moreover, if you ask yourself which picture looks truer to life: profit margins weakening with steady unemployment and growing excess capacity or with steady excess capacity and falling unemployment, I think you will agree it is the first.

If this were the whole story, or the main part of it, a remarkable implication would follow. The distribution of income between wages and profits would be determined essentially by the condition that the saving rate for the economy as a whole be equal to a given number, the investment requirement for steady-state growth, expressed per unit of output. If, for instance, the fraction of wages saved (or the fraction of profits saved) were just equal to vn, the whole of the national income would have to go to wages (or to profits) when the steady state was eventually reached. That does not sound terribly plausible. Nor do distributional shifts of the size one actually sees seem sufficient to do the work this mechanism requires them to do.

There remains the possibility of making the capital/output ratio a variable, and the further possibility of combining a variable capital/output ratio with an endogenously determined saving rate. That is, in fact, what most work on the theory of economic growth actually does, because this line of thought seems to lead to more interesting ideas than any other.

Naturally, I hope they are more than merely 'interesting'. A parable that permits the capital/output ratio to be a variable is actually more plausible than one that does not. Of course, no one has ever seen 'aggregate output' or Net National Product being produced by Aggregate Inputs of Labour and Capital. But if an imaginary world in which this does happen is to provide a tolerable idealization of the real world, then it ought to allow for the possibility of more or less capital-intensive dispositions of resources. Whatever one believes about the flexibility of individual production processes, the economy as a whole has a simple way of moving from capital-poor to capital-rich allocations of resources—by expanding the production of those commodities that are typically produced with lots of capital relative to other resources, and by contracting, at least relatively, the production of commodities that are produced with lots of other resources. There is even a natural way in which this process could come about, provided the cost of the use of capital goods falls relative to the cost of other resources, as capital becomes more abundant. For then the price of capital-intensive goods and services will generally fall compared with the price of others. Even if there is no real possibility of substituting capital for labour and other resources on the production side, there is certainly the possibility of substituting relatively cheap for relatively dear commodities on the consumption side.

International comparisons of national income are notoriously unreliable, and international comparisons of the real stock of capital are probably more so. Nevertheless, for whatever they are worth, Denison's figures exhibit fairly wide variation of the ratio of capital to output among the countries he covers. He shows the U.K. with a capital/output ratio in 1960 about two-thirds that in the U.S. and about half that in Norway.

Suppose we accept it as a fact that the capital/output ratio in our model economy is a variable. That means not only that it can be different at different times—there are very few numbers of which that is not true. It means that, at any given time, it might have been different from what it actually was, and not merely by chance. To tell that story, it is better to start at the beginning, and to enlarge the cast of characters.

2

A Variable Capital/Output Ratio

IN any year, the model economy is equipped with a stock of capital which it has inherited from the past. Within the confines of the model, it is a stock of homogeneous capital goods, saved from past outputs. In a later chapter I will show how that restriction can be lifted, at least a little, to speak of more efficient—usually newer—and less efficient—usually older—capital goods. Given the inherited stock of capital goods, the annual output of the economy depends on the volume of employment. It comes naturally to an economist to draw a curve showing how much output corresponds to each possible level of employment. The curve (see Figure 1) will rise, because more employment, even with the given stock of capital, will produce more output. The curve is likely to be concave: equal successive increments of employment will generate successively smaller increments to output. If capital were truly homogeneous, the curvature would have to be attributed to diminishing returns. It does no harm here to step outside the model and say that more efficient plant and equipment will be drawn into production first, less efficient capacity will be drawn into production later. 'More efficient' can only mean yielding higher output per man, in this short-run macroeconomic context with raw materials ignored and capital goods already there. The result is the same: for the economy as a whole there are diminishing returns to employment.

What happens in the next period? If net investment has taken place, the economy will have more capital at its disposal (and some of it, being very modern, may be very efficient). The new curve relating output to employment will presumably lie wholly above the old curve. The same volume of employment will produce more output one year later than it would have done one year earlier. We have to be more precise than that, if we are to trace out a process of growth of output and capital year after year. We have to know fairly accurately how each year's investment shifts the immediate relation between employment and output.

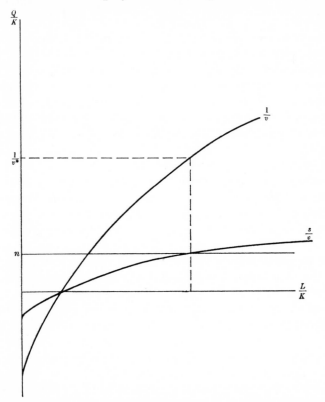

FIG. 1. Determination of steady state with variable capital/ output ratio

Most of the time I will make the simplest—no doubt too simple—assumption that the economy's production possibilities are subject to constant returns to scale in its two homogeneous factors of production, labour and capital: that is to say, if the economy were to employ twice as much, or half as much, capital and labour it merely duplicates at twice the scale or half the scale what it could do before. This means that the economy's production possibilities are summed up in a productivity function that shows how much output per unit of capital is producible for each rate of employment per unit of capital. Think of the unit of capital as a 'factory'. Then the curve for one factory is all we need. What is more, this curve looks exactly like the curve I have already drawn: it starts quite low, perhaps at zero, so that output is negligibly small when employment is negligibly small, no matter how much capital the economy has, more likely at a negative value to allow for the need to make good depreciation before any net output appears. It rises, showing diminishing returns to successive increases in employment, and it ends up quite high.

Output per unit of capital is the reciprocal of the capital/output ratio, so this curve shows, in effect, how the capital/output ratio varies as employment per unit of capital varies. When employment is very low for a given stock of capital, the capital/output ratio is very high, perhaps infinitely high. When employment is very high for a given stock of capital, the capital/output ratio is very low.

We can state all this mathematically. If output (Q) is produced by employment (L) and capital (K) under constant return to scale, we can say that $Q = F(L, K)$, with F homogeneous of degree one. Therefore

$$\frac{1}{v} = \frac{Q}{K} = F\left(\frac{L}{K}, 1\right) = f\left(\frac{L}{K}\right) = f(z) \qquad (1)$$

where z is employment per unit of capital and f is the productivity function referred to in the text and plotted in Figure 1. If we interpret Q as gross output, it is natural to assume $f(0) = 0$. If, as is sometimes more convenient, we interpret Q as net output (after depreciation of capital goods is deducted), one would have to suppose that $f(0) < 0$. In any case, $f' > 0$ (positive marginal product of employment) and $f'' < 0$ (diminishing returns to employment).

Now suppose the economy always saves a constant fraction of its net output. Whenever the economy achieves a given employment per unit of capital it produces a certain output per unit of capital. Its saving and investment per unit of capital is a fraction s of that. We can show that on the diagram by drawing a new curve on which each ordinate of the productivity curve is reduced to the fraction s of itself. This new curve gives the investment per unit of existing capital corresponding to each level of employment per unit of capital. If the capital/output ratio is called v, then output per unit of capital is $1/v$, and the new curve measures s/v for each level of employment.

This is not a statement about cause and effect. If, as Keynes taught, investment is properly regarded as the active element, then the curve shows us (on the horizontal axis) how much employment will be generated by any particular rate of investment (on the vertical axis), given the stock of capital existing. Under the assumptions we are making, capital is unlikely to be idle; short-run fluctuations of output are transmitted wholly to employment. Given the stock of capital, then, any arbitrary rate of investment (per unit of capital) determines a point on the vertical axis. Move horizontally to the intersection with s/v, then vertically upward to $1/v$. The ordinate of that point is the output (per unit of capital) corresponding to the given investment by the ordinary multiplier process. The abscissa is the employment (per unit of capital) corresponding to the determinate output. Draw a horizontal line at the height n, the rate of growth of the labour force. It intersects the saving-investment curve where $n = s/v$, or $s = vn$. At that point and only at that point, the Harrod–Domar consistency condition is satisfied, and the economy is capable of steady-state growth. That is not yet to say it will ever get to a steady state, but only that it can be in one if it should somehow get there. This one and only one possible steady-state configuration fixes the whole picture of the economy, except for its absolute scale. The diagram gives directly the output per unit of capital and the employment per unit of capital; the ratio of those two is the output per head (of employment). The diagram also gives, somewhat less directly, the consumption per unit of capital: that can in turn be converted into consumption per head through division by employment per unit of capital.

The economy need not be in its steady-state configuration. At any moment, its capital stock is whatever past accumulation has made it; its labour supply is whatever its population and participation rate make it, but its labour supply is growing at rate n, by assumption. Somehow, perhaps by an independently determined rate of investment, perhaps otherwise, it arrives at a current output and, accordingly, a current volume of employment (which I assume to be less than the available supply). The height of the s/v-curve gives investment per unit of capital, which is just the rate of growth of the capital stock; the horizontal line at n shows the given rate of growth of the labour force. Anywhere to the right of the steady state, the capital stock is growing faster than the labour force; anywhere to the left, the labour force is growing faster than the capital stock. Only in the steady state are those two rates of growth equal.

Now I want to conduct an artificial experiment. Suppose the economy maintains a constant rate of unemployment; it will sound more cheerful if we describe it as maintaining full employment, but any constant unemployment rate will do for the purpose of the experiment. (A centrally planned economy does this by fiat; a mixed economy might do it approximately by monetary-fiscal policy, though it would take a richer model to describe the process in any detail— it is a little tricky, because the policy mix has to keep the saving rate constant, to stay within the parable.) So long as the unemployment rate is constant, employment must be growing at the same rate as the labour force, n. Start this economy outside the steady state and let it continue to play these full-employment rules of the game. If we start it to the right of the steady state, its stock of capital is growing at a faster rate than n. The ratio of employment to capital must be falling, and the economy is moving to the left along the horizontal axis. We started it with s/v bigger than n; if it maintains a constant unemployment rate, $1/v$ must fall, v must rise. This process must continue so long as s/v exceeds n. Eventually $s/v = n$. The full employment path for this economy tends to the steady state.

If we start the economy to the left of the steady state, the same thing will happen in reverse. To the left of the steady state, s/v is less than n. The capital stock is growing more slowly than employment. The economy is moving to the right along the axis, towards the steady-state point. The capital/output ratio v is decreasing and must continue to decrease so long as s/v falls short of n. The process can only end, eventually, when $s/v = n$, when the steady state is reached. From this side too, all constant-unemployment-rate paths converge on the steady state.

The mathematics of this mechanism is not difficult. Let dots stand for time derivatives, so that, for example, $\dot{v} = dv/dt$. Then, by logarithmic differentiation of (1),

$$-\frac{\dot{v}}{v} = \frac{zf'(z)}{f(z)} \frac{\dot{z}}{z},$$

where $zf'(z)/f(z) = \eta(z)$ is the elasticity of output with respect to employment, always between zero and one. But $\dot{v}/v = (\dot{K}/K) - (\dot{Q}/Q)$ and $\dot{z}/z = (\dot{L}/L) - (\dot{K}/K) = n - (\dot{K}/K)$ along paths with constant unemployment rate. It follows that

$$\frac{\dot{v}}{v} = \frac{\dot{K}}{K} - \frac{\dot{Q}}{Q} = \eta(z)\left(\frac{\dot{K}}{K} - n\right),$$

$$\frac{\dot{Q}}{Q} - n = (1 - \eta(z))\left(\frac{\dot{K}}{K} - n\right).$$

Therefore, the capital/output ratio is rising if and only if output is growing faster than the natural rate (i.e. if and only if the stock of capital is growing faster than employment).

To carry the argument further, let the proportion of output saved be s. Then $\dot{K} = sQ$ and

$$\frac{\dot{z}}{z} = n - \frac{\dot{K}}{K} = n - s\frac{Q}{K} = n - \frac{s}{v}.$$

So z is rising whenever $n > s/v$, falling whenever $n < s/v$, stationary when $n = s/v$. If v is a decreasing function of z, which we assume, and covers a broad enough range, there will be one and only one z, say z^*, at which $n = s/v$. Whenever $z > z^*$, $n < s/v$ and z falls; whenever $z < z^*$, $n > s/v$ and z rises. Thus eventually $z \to z^*$, $v \to 1/\{f(z^*)\}$, and the economy tends to its unique steady-state configuration.

Here, then, is a mechanism that makes steady states possible and accounts, in a way, for the fact that the behaviour we observe seems to be not very far from steady-state in character. It is only a partial explanation; it is a statement about full-employment or constant-unemployment paths, and it says nothing to suggest that capitalist economies will actually follow such paths. I am inclined to think it is appropriate that the model should be silent on this. There were wide swings in unemployment rates in the major industrial capitalist economies during the first 40 years of this century; there have been much narrower swings since the end of the war. The causes of that change are unlikely to find their way into so simple a model as this one, especially not if, as seems likely, a rise in the economic weight of government and in the sophistication of public policy played an important part in bringing it about.

In the steady state, employment, output, and the stock of capital are all growing at the same rate, because they all bear constant ratios to one another. Since one of those rates of growth is exogenously given, it and it alone determines the steady-state rate of growth. In this story, the rate of population growth is the 'natural' rate of growth for the economy.

Figure 2 will tell us easily how changes in the parameters of the economy affect its steady-state configuration. A higher saving-rate, for example, can not affect the ultimate steady-state rate of growth, for that is given by n. The higher saving rate moves the s/v-curve proportionately higher from the position s_1 to s_2 in Figure 2; its intersection with the horizontal at n shifts to the left. This means a lower steady-state ratio of employment to capital. So long as the economy maintains full employment, its aggregate employment is given, proportional to its population and labour force. So it is a bit more informative to say that a steady state with a higher saving-rate will have a higher ratio of capital to

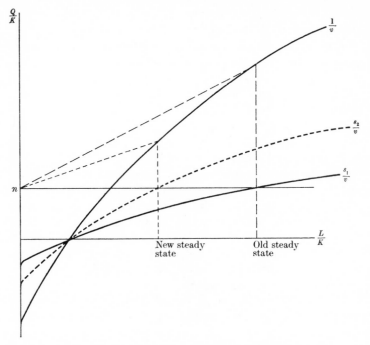

FIG. 2. Effect of a changed saving rate on the steady state

employment. It will generate more capital on which it will employ its given labour force. Output per worker will be higher; output per unit of capital will be lower (i.e. the capital/output ratio will be higher).

Imagine the model economy as having been in a steady state with a saving rate s_1. Output has been growing at the steady proportional rate n. The logarithm of output, shown in the upper panel of Figure 3, has been growing linearly along a straight line with slope n, indexed by the saving rate

s_1. Consumption, which is $(1-s_1)$ times output, has thus been growing at the rate n; its logarithm has been moving along a straight line of slope n indexed by s_1 in the lower panel of Figure 3.

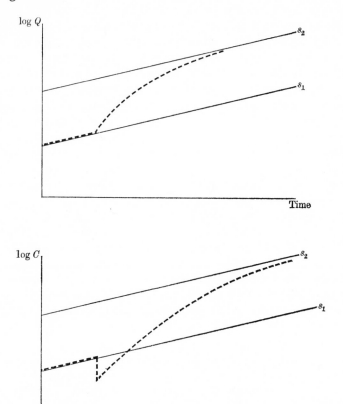

FIG. 3. Time profile with a sudden increase in saving rate

Suddenly the economy begins to save and invest a larger fraction, s_2, of its output. How will it evolve? Immediately after the change, we can forget about the old saving rate s_1; it is responsible for the existing stock of capital at the moment of the change, but it plays no further role. The economy is now not in the steady state corresponding to the new saving rate s_2. Provided it maintains full employment (which may be a tall order), it will move towards the new steady state, for reasons we already know. A moment after the change (see Figure 3) it will be producing a higher output, because it will have accumulated more capital than it would have done at the old saving rate, and its employment is *by assumption* the same as it would have been. (Its consumption per head will be lower, because the increase in s at the initial instant inflicted an immediate reduction in consumption per head.) Initially, then, the rate of growth of output must be higher than the steady-state rate of growth, because output is increasing faster than it did in the old steady state. But eventually the economy approaches its new steady state; the rate of growth of output slows down to the natural rate, the rate of growth of the labour force, because employment per unit of capital, output per unit of capital, and output per man all approach their new steady-state values. The pay-off from the higher saving rate is not a permanently higher rate of growth; it is a permanently higher output per man. (If the increased saving effort were at all worth while, there must presumably be a higher consumption per head in the new steady state, with the initial reduction eventually reversed, despite the higher saving-rate, because of the higher output per head. But we will come to that later.)

If all paths are constant-unemployment-rate paths, the rate of growth will be above or below the steady-state rate of growth whenever the capital/output ratio is rising or falling. But all such paths will eventually settle down into a steady state at the natural rate of growth. Only the ultimate level of the capital/output ratio and output per head depend on the particular constant saving rate.

A change in the other parameter, the rate of population growth, has to be analysed a bit differently, because it does entail a change in the natural rate of growth of output: the two are the same in this model. If we keep this in mind, the rest is easy. An increase or decrease in n is the same as an upward or downward shift of the horizontal line in Fig. 2. Evidently, a faster rate of population growth corresponds to a higher steady-state level of output per unit of capital and employment per unit of capital; a slower rate of population growth reduces output and employment per unit of capital. That is natural enough: an economy with a more rapid growth of population should end up in a less capital-intensive steady state.

It is less clear how consumption per head varies from steady state to steady state, but a little further work on Fig. 2 will let us settle that question too. The vertical distance between the $1/v$-curve and the s/v-curve measures consumption per unit of capital: output per unit of capital less saving per unit of capital. The horizontal coordinate measures employment per unit of capital. The ratio of those two numbers or distances is therefore consumption per worker which, on our present assumptions, we can use as an indicator of consumption per head of population. In any steady state, consumption per head is represented by the slope of a line running from the point n on the vertical axis to the steady-state point on the output-per-unit-of-capital curve.

Hold the natural rate of growth constant and let the saving rate vary. Consumption per head in each possible steady-state is read off from the changing slope of the line anchored at a fixed point on the vertical axis and rotating as its other end moves along the $1/v$-curve. Obviously consumption per head is very low for very low saving-rates, when the steady state is far to the right; diminishing returns to labour accounts for that. Consumption per head is also very low for very high saving-rates, when the steady state is far to the left; diminishing returns to capital accounts for that. The slope of the rotating line, and therefore consumption per head, is at its largest when the line is just tangent to the $1/v$-curve.

What saving rate brings that about? The slope of the $1/v$-curve is the marginal product of labour; it is the increment of output generated by a unit increment of labour with the stock of capital fixed. The tangency-situation makes the marginal product of labour just equal to consumption per head, or the wage bill just equal to total consumption (if the wage is equal to the marginal product of labour, as it would be if the model economy were perfectly competitive). But if the wage bill is equal to total consumption, total profits (the rest of income) must be equal to total investment (the rest of output). Since, in a steady-state total investment is just equal to the rate of growth times the stock of capital, and since, in competitive equilibrium with constant returns to scale, total profits is equal to the marginal product of capital times the stock of capital, another way to describe the maximum-consumption-per-head situation is to say that the marginal product of capital (the competitive rate of profit) must be just equal to the natural rate of growth. All these descriptions are equivalent ways of describing one among the infinitely many steady states.

So long as the saving rate is below the critical value (or, what is the same thing, the marginal product of capital is above the rate of growth) an increase in the saving rate will lead to a steady state with a higher level of consumption per head. Eventually a saving rate high enough to generate the maximum consumption per head is reached, and any further increase in the saving rate will lead back to a steady state with a lower permanent consumption per head. Clearly it will never pay to push saving and investment to such a point that the marginal product of capital falls below the rate of growth for ever. That would be over-saving with a vengeance; for it would lead to a permanent reduction in consumption per head once the steady state were reached. Society would be reducing its consumption merely to support the growth of a capital stock which is so large that diminishing returns have robbed it of its capacity to support its own growth and leave a surplus for extra consumption.

Here, too, the algebra is simple. We know that $1/v = Q/K = f(z)$ is output per unit of capital, and $z = L/K$ is employment per unit of capital. Therefore $\{f(z)\}/z$ is output per head. In a steady state, the capital stock is growing at rate n, so saving and investment is $\dot{K} = nK$ and saving-investment per head is $nK/L = n/z$. So consumption per head is $\{f(z)-n\}/z$. This is maximized among steady states when its derivative with respect to z is zero, i.e. when

$$\frac{n-\{f(z)-zf'(z)\}}{z^2} = 0$$

or when $f(z)-zf'(z) = n$. But $f'(z)$ is the marginal product of employment and $f(z)-zf'(z)$ is the marginal product of capital [because

$$\frac{\mathrm{d}}{\mathrm{d}K} Kf(z)=f(z)-Kf'(z)\frac{L}{K^2} = f(z)-zf'(z)].$$

Therefore the steady state with maximal consumption per head occurs when the marginal product of capital is equal to the natural rate of growth. Then the total of competitively imputed profits is $K\{f(z)-zf'(z)\} = nK = \dot{K}$ equals total saving-investment. The saving rate is the competitively imputed share of profits in total output.

It is less obvious from the diagram that steady-state consumption per head must fall with an increase in the rate of population growth, but it is so. Consumption per head is a ratio, consumption per unit of capital divided by employment per unit of capital. We know that the denominator rises with the rate of population growth; so does the numerator. The fraction will increase only if the numerator rises proportionally more than the denominator, that is, if the elasticity of output per unit of capital with respect to employment per unit of capital is greater than one. But that is never so with constant returns to scale and positive marginal products; a 1 per cent rise in employment, with capital constant, necessarily yields an increase in output smaller than 1 per cent. An economy that must in a steady state support a more rapidly growing population will support it at a lower standard of consumption, given the saving rate.

More rigorously, from the Harrod–Domar condition $sf(z) = n$, we find that $sf'(z)\,\mathrm{d}z/\mathrm{d}n = 1$, or $\mathrm{d}z/\mathrm{d}n = 1/\{sf'(z)\}$.

Clearly higher n goes along with higher steady-state z. Now steady-state consumption per head is $\{f(z)-n\}/z$ and

$$\frac{\mathrm{d}}{\mathrm{d}n}\left(\frac{f(z)-n}{z}\right) = \frac{z\left\{f'(z)\dfrac{\mathrm{d}z}{\mathrm{d}n}-1\right\}-\{f(z)-n\}\dfrac{\mathrm{d}z}{\mathrm{d}n}}{z^2}$$

$$= \frac{z\left(\dfrac{1}{s}-1\right)-\{f(z)-n\}\dfrac{1}{sf'(z)}}{z^2}$$

$$= \frac{z\left(\dfrac{1}{s}-1\right)-\{f(z)-sf(z)\}\dfrac{1}{sf'(z)}}{z^2}$$

$$= \frac{z(1-s)-(1-s)\dfrac{f(z)}{f'(z)}}{sz^2}$$

$$= \frac{1-s}{sz^2}\left\{z-\frac{f(z)}{f'(z)}\right\}.$$

This is clearly negative, since $\{zf'(z)\}/\{f(z)\} < 1$ so long as the marginal product of capital is positive.

So far, I have shown how the assumption that the capital/output ratio is variable can account for the possibility of steady states. With the additional assumption (or 'stylized fact'?) that the unemployment rate fluctuates within fairly narrow limits in modern industrial economies, it turns out that this one-commodity model economy always moves towards its steady state. It is possible, on this basis, to explain why observed economies behave as we have seen that they do. (It hardly needs saying that no one is entitled to leap from this simple parable to explanations of observed economic life. Some reasons for special care will emerge in later lectures. Still, if I did not think the parable contains some of the truth, I would have no excuse for telling the story.)

VARIABLE SAVING RATE AND CAPITAL/OUTPUT RATIO COMBINED

There is no need to limit our exploration of the Harrod–Domar problem to situations in which only one of the three key numbers is an accommodating variable. Both the saving rate and the capital/output ratio are economic variables, even along full employment paths, and both ought to be allowed to vary. Just to show how it is done, I will consider two alternative theories of saving.

The first we have already met; it postulates fixed saving ratios from wage and profit income, a larger one from profits than from wages. The aggregate saving rate is thus a weighted average of the two elementary saving rates. Alternatively, the aggregate saving rate is equal to the saving rate from wages (as a base, so to speak) plus the extra saving from profits, which is the difference between the two saving rates multiplied by the share of profits, the proportion of income subject to the extra saving. Now the share of profits in income is the rate of profit times the capital/output ratio. It follows that $s = s_w + (s_p - s_w)rv$, where r stands for the rate of profit, and therefore $s/v = s_w/v + (s_p - s_w)r$. The same diagram will do duty here, provided we make some definite assumption about the behaviour of the rate of profit. Not much is required. It is adequate if we merely assume that profits increase (or do not decrease) with employment, given the stock of capital, so that in a scale-free economy, the rate of profit is higher (or no lower) the higher the ratio of employment to capital.

This is enough to imply that the new s/v, where s is a composite variable and not a constant, still rises from left to right on the diagram, because both $1/v$ and r rise. The general picture remains the same, and the steady state can be picked out as the solution of $s/v = n$. The rest of the argument applies as before. The new s/v-curve is shifted upward by any increase in s_w or s_p, or by anything that makes the rate of profit higher at each ratio of employment to capital, and the consequences are as they were before, if full employment can be maintained. The capital/output ratio, the rate of profit, and the division of income between wages and profits now depend on economic forces. They will all be constant in any full-employment steady state because their common determinant—the relative scarcity of labour and capital— is constant in a steady state. (I am not using distributional forces to ensure full employment, nor is distribution in this model governed by the satisfaction or failure of the Harrod–Domar condition.)

Any theory of saving that makes the saving rate depend only on the variables of the model—the capital/output ratio, the labour/capital ratio, the return on capital—can be handled in the same way. It is only necessary to keep track of the variations in s, and therefore in s/v. For example, many such theories, however they are phrased, make the saving rate a function of the gap between a desired stock of wealth and the current stock of wealth, both taken relative to current income. The larger the current stock of wealth, compared with the target, the lower is current saving. Within the one-commodity one-asset world of the model, wealth and capital mean the same thing. Such theories boil down, then, to the statement that the saving rate depends on the current capital/output ratio and a target capital/output ratio. The target ratio of wealth to income is usually thought to be an increasing function of the rate of profit on capital.

The higher is the rate of profit, the larger is the target capital/output ratio, and therefore the larger is the saving rate. For given v, s is an increasing function of r. For given rate of profit, the higher is the current capital/output ratio the lower the saving rate, because the gap between desired and actual wealth is smaller. For given r, s is a decreasing function of v. Obviously, then, s/v is an increasing function of r and a decreasing function of v. Under full employment conditions, saving behaviour is such that the stock of capital grows faster the higher is the rate of profit, and the lower is the capital/output ratio. Provided we continue to assume that the rate of profit varies with the relative scarcity of capital in the natural way, the situation is exactly as it was before. The s/v-curve rises, $s/v = n$ in the one and only one

steady-state configuration, and all full employment paths
lead to the steady state. Only the background interpretation
has changed, and then only as regards the determinants of
total saving.

TECHNOLOGICAL PROGRESS

There is, of course, one glaring deficiency in this account
of steady-state behaviour. It accounts for a steady state in
which the ratio of employment to capital is ultimately constant, so the capital stock is growing at the same rate as the
supply of labour. Since the capital/output ratio is also constant—this is one of the defining characteristics of a steady
state—so also aggregate output grows at the same rate as
employment, and output per head is constant. But the facts,
whether stylized or plain, require that both output and the
capital stock grow faster than employment. Modern industrial
economies grow steadily more capital-intensive—in the capi-
tal-per-worker sense—and productivity continues to rise.
Something must have been left out of the model.

There are two obvious candidates: technological progress
and increasing returns to scale. The model so far excludes
them both. There is a once-for-all relation between employment and output, given the stock of capital; and the assumption of constant returns to scale converts that into a once-
for-all relation between employment per unit of capital and
output per unit of capital. It follows that whenever the
capital/output ratio is constant, the capital/labour ratio
must be constant. The introduction of technological progress
would change this: capital and output could both rise through
time faster than employment. Continuous innovation could
stave off the effects of diminishing returns, which otherwise
bring any such process to a halt. Increasing returns to
scale could do the same. The steady enlargement of the scale
of the economy could offset diminishing returns and permit
a continuing rise in capital and output per man.

It is not quite so simple. What I have just said is true.
But closer analysis shows that for all this to happen in steady-
state conditions, with constant rates of growth, the

technological progress must be of a certain form, or the increasing returns to scale must enter in a certain way. The Harrod–Domar condition is particular about the sorts of production conditions it will permit.

I am going to concentrate on technological progress and omit increasing returns. I have two reasons for this choice. In the first place, I reckon that technological progress must be the more important of the two in real economies. It is difficult to believe that the United States is enabled to increase output per man at something over 2 per cent a year mainly by virtue of unexploited economies of scale. This is not to deny the existence of economies of scale, more so in smaller economies than the American, but only to suggest that their effect is probably overshadowed by those of technological progress. Second, it is possible to give theoretical reasons why technological progress might be forced to assume the particular form required for the existence of a steady state. They are excessively fancy reasons, not altogether believable. But that is more of a lead than we have on the side of increasing returns.

The particular form that technological progress must take is called labour-augmenting. There must be a way of measuring employment in 'efficiency-units' so that the underlying technological relation between output and employment for given capital stock is unchanged from year to year *when employment is measured in efficiency units*. If labour is measured in natural units, man-years or man-hours, the input–output relation will shift; the same employment and stock of capital will yield more output in a later year than in an earlier year. In the later year, each man-hour of employment supplies more than 1 man-hour of labour input in efficiency units; and the efficiency-unit content of 1 man-hour rises steadily from year to year. If we are to have exponential growth, then the supply of labour in efficiency units must be growing exponentially.

It should be realized that this reduction of technological change to the efficiency-unit content of an hour of labour is a metaphor. It need not refer to any change in the intrinsic

quality of labour itself. It could in fact be an improvement
in the design of the typewriter that gives one secretary the
strength of 1·04 secretaries after a year has gone by. What
matters is this special property that there should be a way of
calculating efficiency-units of labour, *dependent on the passage
of time but not on the stock of capital*, so that the input–
output curve doesn't change at all in that system of
measurement.

It is not easy to explain why this special labour augmenting form of technological progress is necessary for steady-
state growth to be possible. The general idea is this. Suppose
that technological progress were *both* labour and capital
augmenting. The constant saving rate or steady-state assumption requires output to grow at the same rate as capital
in natural units. But the sort of reasoning I used earlier in
this lecture seems to demand that, in the steady state,
capital and labour grow at the same rate in efficiency units.
But then, under constant returns to scale, output must grow
at that common rate too. So output has to grow at the same
rate as both capital in natural units and capital in efficiency
units. There is evidently trouble unless natural and efficiency
units are the same for capital, and that is the same thing as
saying that technological progress augments labour only.
That is hardly a rigorous argument, but something very like
it is true. (I labour this point slightly, because the presence
of a touch of capital-augmenting technical progress is one of
those nice escape-hatches to be invoked to account for divergences from the steady-state pattern.)

Here is a mathematical argument. Suppose technical progress is both labour- and capital-augmenting, then the production function can be written $Q = F(e^{at}K, e^{bt}L)$. Here
K and L are inputs of capital and labour services in natural
units; but one natural unit of capital supplies e^{at} efficiency-
units of capital services at time t, and one natural unit of
labour provides e^{bt} efficiency-units of labour services at time
t. By constant return to scale, $Q = e^{at}KF\{1, e^{(b-a)t}L/K\}$ and
therefore $1/v = e^{at}f\{e^{(b-a)t}z\}$, where f is the productivity function giving output per unit of capital as a function of

employment per unit of capital. In general, the productivity function shifts through time.

In a steady state, by definition, v is constant, employment grows like e^{nt}, and capital (and output) grow like e^{gt}, where g stands for the natural rate of growth of output and is still to be determined in terms of the other parameters. Therefore $1/v = e^{at}f\{e^{(b-a+n-g)t}\} = e^{at}f(e^{ht})$, with $1/v$ constant and $b-a+n-g = h$ for convenience.

There are now two possiblities. One is that $a = 0$; then $f(e^{ht})$ must be constant. Since $f' > 0$, this implies that $h = 0$, or $b-a+n-g = b+n-g = 0$. This is the case of purely labour-augmenting technical progress ($a = 0$, $b > 0$), and the natural rate of growth of output is the rate of growth of employment in efficiency units, i.e. the sum of the rate of population growth and the rate of labour-augmenting technical progress ($g = n+b$). Since $a = 0$, we have $1/v = f(e^{bt}z)$, and $e^{bt}z = e^{bt}L/K = \bar{z}$ is employment in efficiency units per unit of capital. In those units $1/v = f(\bar{z})$ and the productivity function is invariant through time.

The other possibility is that a is not zero. Since $1/v = e^{at}f(e^{ht})$ for all t, we can differentiate with respect to time and rearrange to get

$$\frac{a}{n} = \frac{e^{ht}f'(e^{ht})}{f(e^{ht})}$$

The left-hand side is constant; set $e^{ht} = u$, so that u ranges over all positive values, and observe that $\{uf'(u)\}/\{f(u)\}$ must be a constant, say η. From this, two things follow. First, $-a/(b-a+n-g) = \eta$, so $g = b+n+(1-\eta)a/\eta$. Second $f(u) = Au^{\eta}$, so the full production function is

$$Q = Ae^{at}K\left\{e^{(b-a)t}\frac{L}{K}\right\} = A(e^{at}K)^{1-\eta}(e^{bt}L)^{\eta},$$

namely a Cobb–Douglas function. But this can equally well be written

$$Q = AK^{1-\eta}\left\{e^{\left(b+\frac{1-\eta}{\eta}a\right)t}L\right\}^{\eta}$$

In the Cobb–Douglas case, with constant η, technical progress can *always* be thought of as purely labour augmenting at the rate $b+\{(1-\eta)/\eta\}a$. When that is done, the formula for g is just as in the labour-augmenting case. So there is really only one case after all.

Provided technological change is labour augmenting, there is no problem in completing the analysis. We need only reinterpret the standard diagram in two ways. First, measure on the horizontal axis employment in efficiency units per unit of capital. Then the $1/v$ and s/v curves have the same meaning as before, output per unit of capital and saving-investment per unit of capital at full employment, since output and capital are measured in natural units as they were before. Second, draw the horizontal line at a height equal to the rate of growth of employment in efficiency units (g, say) which will be the sum of the natural increase in labour force, and the rate of labour-augmenting technological progress (i.e. the rate at which the efficiency content of a man-year of labour is rising through time).

Now as before, s/v is the rate of growth of the stock of capital. To the left of the steady-state intersection, the capital stock is growing more slowly than employment in efficiency units, so the horizontal coordinate is increasing. To the right of the intersection, the stock of capital is growing more rapidly than employment in efficiency units per unit of capital, so the horizontal coordinate is decreasing. In the end, the economy tends to the intersection, where the stock of capital and 'effective' employment are growing at the same rate, the capital/output ratio is constant, $s = vg$, and the economy is in a steady state.

In this steady state, the stock of capital is growing faster than employment in natural units; the excess rate of growth is equal to the rate of labour-augmenting technological progress. Since the capital/output ratio is constant, output per man is also growing at the rate of technological progress. The main defect in the picture of the steady state has been repaired.

The analysis of the effects of changes in parameters is more or less unchanged. The natural rate of growth is now the sum of the rate of population increase and the rate of technological progress. A change in the saving rate does not change that; it changes bodily the whole curve of output per man and consumption per man, both of which are rising at the rate of technological progress. The only additional fact worth noting is that an increase in the rate of technological progress itself, besides increasing the rates of growth of output and output per head (and therefore consumption per head), will also increase effective employment per unit of capital, and will therefore increase the steady-state rate of profit under the broad assumption I have been using.

All this is under the convenient assumption that technological progress is labour augmenting. If that is not the case, there is no steady-state configuration. The Harrod–Domar consistency condition can not be permanently satisfied. It is worth mentioning what will happen if there is some capital augmenting technological progress. A constant saving-rate and a constant capital/output ratio are incompatible. If the economy maintains full employment (or a constant unemployment rate) with a constant fraction of output saved and invested, the capital/output ratio will persistently rise and the rate of profit will persistently fall. If the economy wishes to—or thinks it must—maintain a constant rate of profit and a constant capital/output ratio, it must save and invest a persistently decreasing fraction of its output.

3

A Model without Direct Substitution

THE model I used in the previous chapters is vulnerable to two strong and related objections. (1) Even in the absence of technological progress, it presupposes the existence of a stock of homogeneous capital capable of being operated with more or less labour to produce more or less output. The story then tells how such an economy, if it always employs a fixed fraction of an exponentially growing labour force, and if it saves and invests a fraction of its output determined in some plausible way, will eventually be driven into a steady state. That is to say, its output, employment (in efficiency units) and capital stock will all come to grow at the same rate. Common sense urges, however, that very labour-intensive production and very little-labour-intensive production require different kinds of capital goods.

(2) The presence of technological progress makes things worse. Casual observation suggests that invention rarely takes the form of a discovery that permits the same number of workers with the same amount of identical capital goods to produce a larger output. That would assimilate all or most technological progress to the invention of touch-typing. More often, an invention changes the form of the capital goods used in production; it leads to the electric typewriter or the diesel engine, or something of the sort.

In either case, the story of the approach to steady-state growth (or, if there is capital-augmenting technological progress, a definite kind of divergence from the steady state) breaks down in two ways. In the first place, an economy approaching the steady state from one side or the other must not merely move to more or less labour-intensive modes of production, it must somehow transform a capital stock appropriate to labour-intensive production into one appropriate to less labour-intensive production, by abandoning the first kind (or letting it wear out without replacement) and constructing the new kind. This process will certainly look different in the short run; and we have no guarantee that even in the long run the story will come out as it did before. More fundamentally, the whole story deals with changes in the ratio of employment to capital or output to capital, and this kind of story seems to make no sense in the more realistic context. How are we to know whether two mixed bags of capital goods, old and new, or labour-intensive and not so labour-intensive, represent the same amount of capital, or which is bigger? If capital goods are not all alike, it may be illegitimate to talk of a stock of capital.

In this chapter I intend to re-work the whole model under extreme assumptions of just the other kind. There will be as many different kinds of capital goods as there are instants of time. I will call these different kinds of capital goods 'vintages', and will label each vintage by the date at which it was itself produced. A unit of capital goods of a given vintage will provide a certain capacity to produce output, and require a fixed amount of labour to produce it, and these characteristics remain unchanged throughout the life of the capital goods. Technological progress is going on steadily, as newer capital goods, i.e. capacity of a later vintage, will always be more efficient, in a well-defined sense, than capacity of an earlier vintage, represented by older capital goods.

One of the advantages of this formulation is that it will allow the model to describe something that the original model could not, namely obsolescence of capital. I will assume, for simplicity, that capital goods last for ever, so far as their physical characteristics are concerned. But they may, and will, become economically useless, not because they wear out, but because they become incapable of covering their costs, of earning positive rents. This was excluded from the earlier model, even in the presence of technological progress, because all capital goods, old and new alike, shared equally in technological progress. Since all capital was homogeneous, none could become obsolete because all would become obsolete.

This is a much harder kind of model to work with, precisely because there is no longer a meaningful stock of capital whose numerical magnitude can be studied. Consequently, I will not be able to argue the case rigorously. The work has been done,[1] but all I will be able to give is a summary view of the outcome.

The main result is that the long-run behaviour of this more complicated economy is very much like that of the simpler economy we have already studied. There is an analogue of the Harrod–Domar consistency condition which must be satisfied in any steady state. The key accommodating variable that moves (or may move) to permit a steady state is not the capital/output ratio; there is no capital/output ratio. It is, instead, the economic lifetime of capital, the length of time that elapses between the moment that investment occurs and the moment at which the capacity laid down becomes obsolete.

In the steady state, the economic lifetime is constant; each successive vintage of capital becomes obsolete after μ years of operation. Outside the steady state, the economic lifetime varies from one vintage to the next. In the simpler economy, a steady state is possible with given rates of population growth and labour augmenting technological progress but different saving rates, because the higher saving-rate corresponds to a higher capital/output ratio and a lower ratio of employment in efficiency-units to stock of capital. In this model, the steady state with the higher saving rate corresponds to a shorter economic lifetime; the greater volume of saving is accommodated by faster obsolescence. (Parallel statements hold for higher and lower rates of population growth. In one model, faster growth of employment is accommodated by higher employment in efficiency units per unit of capital, that is, by more labour-intensive production; in

[1] See R. Solow, J. Tobin, C. C. von Weizsäcker, and M. E. Yaari: 'Neoclassical Growth with Fixed Factor Proportions', *Review of Economic Studies*, XXXIII (April 1966) 79–115.

the other model by slower obsolescence.) In both cases, there have to be corresponding changes in the rate of profit, and that may be a difficult adjustment for a capitalist economy to make while it maintains full employment.

The similarity goes further. It turns out that, even in this more complicated, apparently more rigid, type of economy, all full-employment paths tend to the steady state. That is, if the economy starts off with arbitrary initial conditions (that is, with any prehistory of past investments), but maintains a perpetually constant unemployment rate and saves and invests a constant fraction of its output, it will be driven ultimately to a steady state. Once it is in the steady state, the economic lifetime of capacity will be appropriately constant, and output per man will be growing at the rate of labour-augmenting technological progress. A man from Mars, observing only steady states, would find it hard to tell one kind of economy from the other.

Is it worth the trouble? Well, it is important to know that this kind of multiplicity of capital goods and the absence of smooth substitutability of labour for capital do not alter the main long-run results of the theory. Moreover, it is possible that the interpretation you would put on any real economy would be different in important respects according as you tried to fit the crude facts into one kind of model or the other.

It needs to be said, however, that this model allows only a deceptively simple kind of multiplicity of capital goods. Only one kind of capital goods is constructed at any moment, because the 'latest model' dominates all others. When there are many kinds of capital goods being built at each instant, considerably deeper and more difficult problems arise, and the outcome of the story may be very different. These problems are still unsettled, and I will not be able to discuss them. When we come to consider a monetary economy, however, we will get a glimpse of what can go wrong.

The modified parable goes like this. At any time, the economy employs a certain number of workers $N(t)$ and produces a certain output $Y(t)$. It consumes part of the output and saves and invests the rest, $I(t)$. I shall assume the saving

ratio is constant, so $I(t) = sY(t)$. The investment of one unit
of output creates a units of capacity. If a were an increasing
function of time, there would be capital-augmenting technological progress. Except for an occasional side remark, I
shall assume that technological progress is purely labour-
augmenting, so a is constant. It takes $b_0 e^{-bt}$ men to operate
one unit of capacity of vintage t, i.e. constructed at time t.
Thus b is the rate of labour-augmenting technical progress.
New capital is more efficient than old, but solely in the sense
that output per man is higher for men working in new factories than in old ones; output per man in a factory of vintage
v is $b_0^{-1}e^{bv}$. But once an investment is made, once a factory
is built, output per man in it is constant for the rest of its
life. It might be more natural to suppose that by building
more expensive capacity it would be possible to have a
higher output per man at any point in time; then it would
be possible to substitute higher initial cost for lower operating
cost, or lower initial cost for higher operating cost. By assuming away that possibility, I ensure that at any time everyone builds only the latest-model factory.

The investment of time t thus creates $aI(t)$ of new capacity,
which is capable, if it is actually operated, of employing
$ab_0 e^{-bt} I(t)$ men per year.

At any time, the economy has available whatever amounts
of capacity were created in the past, in the whole past in fact
since I am assuming that capital lasts for ever. The economy
also has available a given supply of labour, which is growing
geometrically at the rate n. How will the economy allocate
its labour to its available capacity?

A planned economy would obviously proceed first by
manning its newest capacity; then, if there were some labour
left over, it would man its next newest capacity; then, if
there were still some labour left over, it would man its next
newest capacity; and so on, until it had allocated all its
labour. In that way, a planned economy would maximize
its output; if there were some older capacity being operated
while some newer capacity were idle, the economy could
increase output by shifting labour from the older to the newer

capacity, from a factory with lower output per man to a factory with higher.

A competitive profit-maximizing economy with flexible real wages would do exactly the same. An old factory would be operated only if the real wage were less than or equal to its output per man; if the real wage were to exceed its output per man, it would be paying out in wages more than its total product—its owners would be earning negative quasi-rents and they would do better to shut down. But then if any older factory were operating while a newer one were idle, the owners of the newer factory could afford to bid labour away from the old one, and would try to do so because they could earn positive quasi-rents even if they bid the real wage up to the point where the older factory fell just below the margin of profitability. Generally speaking, whatever output the economy is producing, the real wage will be bid up to the point where it is just equal to the output per man in the oldest factory in use, for if it were any lower some idle factory would try to get into the act by bidding for labour that it could profitably use, and if it were any higher the profitable capacity would not be enough to produce that output. Thus, if the oldest capacity in use is $\mu(t)$ years old at time t, we must have $w(t) = b_0^{-1}e^{b(t-\mu(t))}$. The capital of age $\mu(t)$, i.e. of vintage $t-\mu(t)$ is no-rent capital, exactly analogous to no-rent land in Ricardian theory. (If business demanded a fixed excess of price over marginal-and-average cost—a constant degree of monopoly—then the real wage would be a fixed fraction of output per man in the oldest factory in use.)

All this can be represented on a diagram (Figure 4). The horizontal axis measures employment, the vertical axis output per man. For time t, construct a rectangle whose base is the total employment required to man the capacity of vintage t, already specified as $ab_0e^{-bt}I(t)$, and whose height is output per man in factories of vintage t, already specified as $b_0^{-1}e^{bt}$. The area of the rectangle is $aI(t)$, the capacity represented by the most recent investment. Construct a similar rectangle for vintage $t-1$, and stand it next to the one for vintage t. Its height will be less by a factor representing the rate of labour-augmenting technological progress. The length of its base will depend on how much investment took place at time $t-1$: the base will be longer than that for

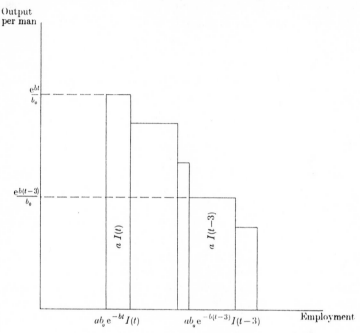

FIG. 4. Employment and productivity for successive
vintages of investment

time t if the volume of investment were constant, because the same amount of lower-productivity capacity will require more employment to operate it.

Do the same for all past vintages, so that we have a sequence of rectangles of diminishing height and perhaps irregular base. (If the unit time interval is very short, or if we go over to continuous time, we have a falling smooth curve instead of a series of rectangles.) Now draw a vertical line on the horizontal axis at the point corresponding to total employment at time t (see Figure 5). The combined area of the boxes to the left of that vertical (or the area under the curve to the left) measures the total output produced by that volume of employment. (Alternatively, if you know the output for time t, slide a vertical line to the right until it cuts off an area equal to that output to its left, and that gives the employment corresponding to the given output.) The

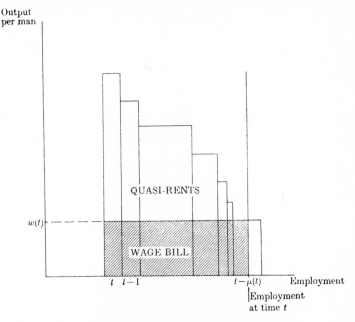

FIG. 5. Income distribution in a vintage model

height of the box (or the curve) corresponding to total employment is the competitive real wage corresponding to that output and employment. Draw a horizontal line at that height: the area of the rectangle under that line is the total wage bill; the remaining area, output less wage bill, is total profits or quasi-rents. Notice that at any time older capital is earning a lower quasi-rent per worker than newer capital, because it pays the same wage and has a lower output per man. It also earns a lower quasi-rent per unit of capacity or per unit of original investment cost.

This tells something about the history of a single factory. When it is new it earns profits equal to the difference between its productive capacity and its wage bill. As it ages, its productive capacity is unimpaired and its output per man is unchanged. But if, as is normal, the real wage rises through time because of technological progress and the competition of newer and more efficient factories, its wage bill will rise and its profits will diminish. Eventually the wage rises as high as the output per man in this factory and it has become the marginal no-rent factory. Let the wage go a touch higher, and this factory goes out of business; it has become obsolete, not because of any reduction in its efficiency, but because the rising real wage has rendered it incapable of covering its own variable costs of production. If the real wage should happen to fall, the factory might come back into operation, but presumably only temporarily until the wage rises out of reach again. In a more complicated model, a factory might lose efficiency during its lifetime; and it would wear out eventually, regardless of the wage.

You can study this process by seeing how the diagram changes from one period to the next. In the next period, a certain amount of gross investment takes place. It generates new capacity whose productivity per man is about $100b$ per cent higher than that of this year's new capacity. A new rectangle is added to the left of the previous ones, with a base equal to the amount of employment the new capacity provides when fully manned. Total employment is now measured from the beginning of that rectangle. In the normal course of events, unless gross investment is particularly small or current employment particularly high, next year's total employment will come to a point on the horizontal axis to the left of last year's point (with each measured from its own origin, of course). In that case the oldest vintage in use last year will have dropped wholly or partially out of production. The real wage will have risen (or at worst stayed the same). In exceptional cases, the margin separating active from idle capacity may move to the right, in which case the real wage can fall and previously retired stand-by capacity may be called back into use. (If it strikes you as odd that a burst of high employment should be accompanied by a reduced real wage, you can take one (or all) of three tacks. (a) The money wage may well rise rapidly but, under competitive assumptions, the commodity price level will have to rise even faster to reduce the real wage, to induce employers to man relatively inefficient productive capacity. (b) If there is a monopolistic margin of price over marginal cost, it may be at least

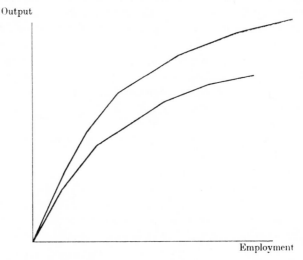

Fɪɢ. 6. Successive total-produce curves for a vintage model

temporarily eroded so that higher employment is compatible with a higher real wage. (c) The actual short-run course of events may depend more on the various lags in the adjustment of wages, prices, employment, production, sales, and inventories than on anything else; only after things have settled down will matters be as I have described them.)

There is another sort of diagram (Figure 6) related to this one as a total product curve is related to a marginal-product curve. This time plot cumulative employment horizontally and total output vertically. When employment is very small, only the newest, most efficient, capacity is used and output rises proportionally with employment, with slope equal to output per man on the newest capacity, i.e. $b_0^{-1}e^{bt}$. When employment has reached the level required to exhaust the capacity of the newest vintage, further employment must be diverted to the next-newest vintage, so there is a corner in the total-product curve. Its slope falls to $b_0^{-1}e^{b\,(t-1)}$, output per man in factories of last year's vintage. The new line segment lasts until last year's vintage is exhausted, and the curve has another corner. The length of each segment depends on how big investment was in the year in question, and on its labour requirement per unit of output. This curve relates output and employment; its slope plays the role of—in fact, is—the marginal product of labour, and gives the competitive real wage corresponding to each level of output and employment. Exactly at the corners, the slope is indeterminate between the slope of the left-hand and that of the right-hand line segments that meet at the corner. (If the margin between active and idle capacity were to fall exactly between two vintages, the real wage could be anything between output per man on the idle vintage and output per man on the active one. Any such wage would be high enough to keep the excluded vintage from bidding profitably for labour, but low enough to yield a profit to the last included vintage.) If the time interval is made small, this polygonal line becomes a smooth curve.

A year goes by and a new vintage appears, more productive than last year's. The new curve leaves the origin with a steeper line segment because output per man is $100b$ per cent higher than it was on last year's newest capacity. When that first line segment comes to an end, the rest of the new curve can be drawn simply by making a new origin at the end point and drawing in last year's curve, transposed bodily to the new origin. (It can be done so simply because no physical depreciation takes place.) The same story can be told using either diagram, so I shall not repeat it.

The internal working of this model certainly differs from the smooth substitution of the more traditional model. Nevertheless, its long-run growth properties are surprisingly similar. The full analysis is rather messy, but I shall go as far as simple reasoning will take me.

STEADY STATES IN THIS MODEL

The first question on the agenda is about the possibility of a steady state. Since there is no 'stock of capital' in this model, we can not talk about the constancy of the capital/output ratio. A steady state will now simply be a situation in which output and employment grow exponentially and a constant fraction of output is consumed, the rest saved. (I talk only about gross saving and investment, because net concepts are also rather difficult in this model in which capital goods become obsolete instead of wearing out.) Can such a situation persist for arbitrary values of the various constants?

If it can, the output of the economy can be represented by $Y_0 e^{gt}$ for some rate of growth g and initial output Y_0. Gross investment must then be $I(t) = s Y_0 e^{gt}$. As before, the labour force and, by assumption, the volume of employment is growing at rate n, so employment is $N_0 e^{nt}$. At any instant of time, total employment must increase by $n N_0 e^{nt}$. The extra workers can occupy brand new factories, which have a capacity of $as Y_0 e^{gt}$ and can provide employment for $b_0 as Y_0 e^{(g-b)t}$ workers. But some of those jobs are needed for workers displaced from factories just passing over the margin into idleness or obsolescence. How many displaced workers are there? If the economic lifetime of capital were constant, they would be the men employed in the factories built exactly μ years ago, and there would be $b_0 e^{-b(t-\mu)} as Y_0 e^{g(t-\mu)}$ of them. If the economic lifetime is changing, that contributes $-b_0 e^{-b(t-\mu)} as Y_0 e^{g(t-\mu)} \, d\mu/dt$ (with a minus sign because a lengthening of the lifetime does not displace, but absorbs, labour). If the unemployment rate is not to rise or fall perpetually, the increment to the supply of labour must be just offset by employment on newly-produced capital, net of those jobs required for displaced workers. Thus

$$n N_0 e^{nt} = a b_0 s Y_0 e^{(g-b)t} \{1 - e^{-(g-b)\mu}(1 - d\mu/dt)\}.$$

Can this equation be satisfied? There are two possibilities: one is that μ is constant and $\mathrm{d}\mu/\mathrm{d}t$ is zero, the other is that μ is changing perpetually. In the first case, the left-hand side is growing exponentially at rate n, the right-hand side at rate $g-b$. It must be, then, that $g = b+n$, the rate of growth of output is the sum of the rate of growth of employment and the rate of labour-augmenting technological progress. That sounds familiar. In addition, it must be so that

$$nN_0 = ab_0 s Y_0 (1-\mathrm{e}^{-n\mu}).$$

Since N_0 is given and I shall soon show how μ is determined, this equation merely fixes Y_0, the level of the output path.

The other case of varying μ can be ruled out; it can be shown to imply that μ either increases indefinitely through time or decreases to zero. If it increases, the economy must eventually run out of capacity and be unable to employ its labour (unless there exists an infinite amount of idle capacity, which is absurd). If it decreases towards zero, gross investment would eventually exceed gross output, which is absurd too.

It follows that the economic lifetime of capital must be constant in a steady state. It remains to determine the economic lifetime corresponding to given values of the constants. We have accounted for employment; we must now account for output. The increase in output at time t is $(n+b) Y_0 \mathrm{e}^{(n+b)t}$. The increase in output is also the capacity in the newest vintage of factories less the capacity passing out of use through obsolescence, $aI(t)-aI(t-\mu) = as Y_0 \mathrm{e}^{(n+b)t} - as Y_0 \mathrm{e}^{(n+b)(t-\mu)}$. (We already know that μ is constant.) It must be the case, therefore, that

$$(n+b) Y_0 \mathrm{e}^{(n+b)t} = as Y_0 \mathrm{e}^{(n+b)t} (1-\mathrm{e}^{-(n+b)\mu}),$$

or

$$g = (n+b) = sa (1-\mathrm{e}^{-(n+b)\mu}).$$

This condition for a steady state involves only μ, the lifetime, and the constants of the model, n, b, a, s. It determines μ or, more precisely, it says what μ has to be in a steady state.

In this model, evidently, the economic lifetime is the variable that has to adjust if arbitrary values of the parameters are to be consistent with steady-state behaviour. Indeed, the condition we have just derived is a consistency condition. It looks very much like the Harrod–Domar condition; in fact it *is* the Harrod–Domar condition for this sort of model. We are used to the Harrod–Domar condition in the form $g = s/v$. The new condition has the same structure if only $1/v$ is replaced by $a\,(1-e^{-g\mu})$. There is obviously some dimensional resemblance since a stands for the output producible by one unit of investment while $1/v$ stood for output per unit of homogeneous capital.

Is there always an economic lifetime satisfying the consistency condition? As μ ranges from zero to infinity, the factor $(1-e^{-g\mu})$ ranges from zero to one. The condition can always be satisfied by one and only one value of μ, unless sa is less than g, in which case it can not be satisfied at all. The badly-behaved case occurs when the labour force in efficiency units is growing so rapidly and the saving rate is so small that the economy is incapable of providing employment for everyone. No matter how long it keeps its capital in service, even infinitely long, its population outruns its ability to generate new capacity and employment opportunities. That case need not detain us. (It was ruled out in the smooth-substitution model by the quick assumption that the curve of output per unit of capital became ultimately 'very high'; notice here that a large enough value of a can always make sa exceed g.)

Apart from this exceptional, but not very likely, case, there is a steady state corresponding to any given values of the technological parameters, saving rate, and rate of population growth. Each different steady state can be characterized by the constant economic lifetime of capital ruling within it. From that relation we can deduce most of what we need to know about the effects of changes in the underlying parameters.

Before I go on to some sample results, there is a second issue to be settled. In the traditional model it was easy to show that the steady state was more than a possibility, but was even a likely state of affairs. An economy that started anywhere, however unbalanced its resources, and under instruction only to maintain a constant unemployment rate and to save a constant fraction of its net income—more general saving rules would do—would necessarily transform itself ultimately into the steady state appropriate to its saving behaviour. The same question has to be asked of the new model. The answer turns out to be the same, though it is this time far from easy to prove it.

This time you have to imagine the economy at time zero, say, having experienced in the past some arbitrary and irregular history of gross investments. The capacity resulting from this history is all still there, the more recent factories more efficient in a labour-augmenting way, the older ones less efficient. There is a lot of capacity of some vintages, when there happened to be investments booms, and rather little capacity of other vintages, dating from days when gross investment was very small. But, from time zero on, the economy is supposed to employ all, or a fixed fraction, of its exponentially growing labour force; it is supposed to consume a fixed fraction of whatever output the labour force produces when it is efficiently distributed over the job lot of available capacity. The remaining fraction of gross output becomes gross investment, and so on to the next instant of time.

In the course of this process, the economic lifetime of capital may behave quite erratically, and so will the competitive real wage. Under the rules of the game, the margin separating active from idle capacity moves as it must to employ the labour force after the newest capacity has been manned. It may therefore jump sharply when the margin passes through a sparse vintage, so that many years of gross investment have to be activated or idled in order to absorb or displace a given number of workers. Output may change erratically too, although employment grows steadily, because the average productivity of labour depends on the age distribution of the capacity being operated. Nevertheless, it is a theorem that this kind of economy, playing the constant-unemployment-and-constant-saving-ratio rules of the game, will transform itself from arbitrary initial conditions into the steady state appropriate to its saving rate, its technology, and its demographic conditions. So in this model too the steady state is not a mere curiosity. It is worth looking more closely at the characteristics of steady-state behaviour.

In fact, a steady state in this model looks just like a steady state in the old model. We already know that output is growing geometrically at a 'natural' rate which is equal to the rate at which employment is growing plus the rate of labour-augmenting technical progress. Output per person, therefore, is growing at the rate of technological progress. There is no capital/output ratio, rigorously speaking; but since investment is a fixed share of output and the lifetime of capital is not changing, any reasonable computation in value terms will show that capital values are rising at the same rate as total output. The competitive real wage is just equal to the output per man characteristic of factories built exactly μ years ago, because those factories must be promptly forced into idleness. So the real wage at time t is $b_0^{-1}e^{b(t-\mu)}$; it is increasing by $100b$ per cent a year, at the same rate as output per man. Employment is increasing at the rate n, so the wage bill for the whole economy is increasing at the rate $n+b$, the same as total output. In the steady state, therefore, the wage bill is a constant fraction of output (but exactly what fraction it is depends on the parameters, both directly and through μ).

A brand new unit of investment produces its capacity output a. To do so it employs, as we have seen, ab_0e^{-bt} men per year. In its first year the wage is $b_0^{-1}e^{b(t-\mu)}$, so it pays out the amount $ae^{-b\mu}$ in wages and earns for its owners $a(1-e^{-b\mu})$ in profits or quasi-rents. It is interesting that these first-year profits are independent of calendar time. Indeed the quasi-rents for any factory depend only on its *age*, not on its birthdate. As a factory ages, its output remains unchanged, and it requires the same number of workers. But the real wage is rising steadily at $100b$ per cent a year; so it earns steadily lower profits. Eventually, indeed precisely at age μ, the profits fall to zero and the factory is retired as obsolete. The rate of profit can be defined as the rate of discount that reduces the stream of profits to a present value of one, which is the initial cost of a unit of investment.

It really only remains to consider changes in parameters and the corresponding changes in steady states. The key to

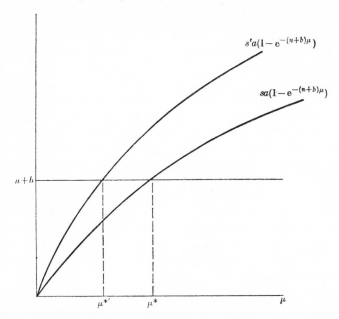

FIG. 7. Steady-state economic lifetime of capital with different saving rates

such questions is the modified Harrod–Domar condition. Some of them can be answered just by looking at a diagram (Figure 7) in which the analogue of s/v, namely $sa(1-e^{-(n+b)\mu})$, is plotted against μ. The answers generally correspond to common sense and the economist's instinct, which may be the same thing.

For example, a higher saving-rate leaves the rate of growth unchanged but shortens the economic lifetime of capital; it does so because—with constant unemployment—there is more new capital to compete with old capital and rob it of its labour. Since capital retires younger, the efficiency of the marginal capital at any time will be higher, so the real wage will be higher, to force it into retirement. The initial profits of a new factory are thus lower, it survives a shorter time, so naturally the rate of profit is lower, and so is the share of profits in total output. You understand this model if you realize that output per man will be higher, averaged over the whole economy, not because 'capital' has been substituted for labour in any direct way, but because the capacity in use is on the average younger and therefore, on the average, more efficient.

The diagram does not speak so unambiguously about an increase in the rate of population growth, because both the curve and the horizontal line shift. The common-sense answers hold, however. A faster rate of population growth prolongs the economic lifetime of capital; the margin must be pushed back to provide employment for the larger labour force. Thus faster growth in the labour force favours a higher rate of profit and a lower real wage. A faster rate of technological progress can be shown to go along with a higher rate of profit in this model; but it makes less sense to talk about its effect on the real wage, because the rate of growth of the real wage changes too.

It is an interesting sidelight that a faster rate of technical progress actually prolongs the lifetime of capital in this particular model, though that is not a general truth. There are offsetting forces at work: faster technological change means that outout grows faster, the volume of new investment grows faster, and this extra competition tends to shorten the lifetime of any given plant. On the other hand, the faster technological progress means that any given amount of new capacity provides fewer jobs, and this tends to keep capacity in service longer to maintain the required amount of employment. For this special model, the second force is stronger and the longer lifetime increases the rate of profit.

There is more to be squeezed out of this model, and for many purposes it is worth squeezing. But my purpose is really the opposite. Since I am concerned mainly with the very long-run steady-state properties of a growing economy, I have salved my conscience and can return to the simpler traditional model. I can do this because I have verified that the two models are really alike from this very-long-run point of view. It is in the transitions that they work rather differently, and this one probably tells a more realistic story.

4

A Model with Two Assets

THE moral of my last chapter was that, so long as we stick to a one-commodity one-asset world, the assumption of a rather more complicated technology does not much change the general character of the results. When there is smooth substitutability of labour for capital, the description of the approach of full-employment-constant-saving-rate paths to a steady state is much simpler than when there is not. The possibility of operating existing capital goods more or less labour-intensively diminishes the hold of past irregularities of investment over the present. But ultimately the result is the same. Ultimately, both kinds of economies, wherever they start, will move towards satisfaction of the Harrod–Domar condition if full employment is maintained and a constant fraction of full-employment output is saved and invested. The steady state, when it is reached, will look much the same in the two kinds of economies; it would be hard to tell which was which merely from the national income statistics, though the life-story of a single factory is in fact rather different in the two economies.

In this chapter I will go back to the simpler technology in which all capital goods are alike. But I will complicate the story in a different way. There will still be only one produced commodity, which can be consumed directly or accumulated as capital to be combined with labour in the production of more of itself. But there will be a second asset, a debt instrument issued by the government, which individuals can hold as a store of wealth. You can think of this paper asset as money, or as government bonds, or as a hybrid. A more complete model would have both interest-bearing and non-interest-bearing government debt, but I will combine them.

Sometimes I will imagine that the government pays interest on its debt, just to give it an extra policy tool. Sometimes you can imagine that interest rate fixed at zero, in which case it is more natural to speak of the debt as money. But it is 'outside' money, in the sense that it is an asset to the private economy unmatched by any private liability.

There are two broad reasons for generalizing the model in this way. It is an obvious step towards realism. Modern economies are monetary economies, and we are entitled to ask whether this fact has any important influence on the real characteristics of a growing economy. In effect, we can study whether money is 'neutral'—not in the old quantity-theory sense of whether doubling the stock of money has any permanent effect beyond a doubling of the nominal price level, but in the related sense of whether doubling the rate of growth of the money supply has any permanent effect beyond doubling the rate of inflation.

Secondly, if we are ever to get beyond studying the characteristics of full employment paths, it will have to be in the context of a monetary economy. Only then does it make sense to talk, as we always do, about the separation of saving and investment decisions. If the only asset available is real capital, or titles to real capital, then every act of saving, i.e. every decision to add to wealth, is a decision to buy real capital, to invest, because there is no other asset to buy.

The technology of the economy is as it was before: output per unit of capital, the reciprocal of the capital/output ratio, is a smoothly increasing, concave, function of employment per unit of capital. That is to say, there are constant returns to scale, positive marginal products of labour and capital, and diminishing returns to both. We can allow labour-augmenting technical progress and measure employment in efficiency units, so that the economy's supply of labour is increasing at a rate equal to the sum of the rate of population growth and the rate of technical progress.

The government levies taxes, makes transfer payments, and buys goods and services, which it uses for some kind of public consumption that does not effect private decisions to spend. Whenever expenditures exceed revenues, the government covers its deficit by issuing the appropriate amount of debt (i.e. by printing money); whenever the government is in surplus it retires debt. (It would serve no purpose for me to worry about what would happen if the government tried to run a surplus when it had no debt outstanding. I shall just assume that contingency away.)

The national accounts of this economy will show a net national product equal to Q in real terms and pQ in current prices, where p is the current money price of a unit of output. Suppose government consumption is a fraction h of net national product; then the government's budget deficit is $hpQ + \text{transfers} - \text{taxes} = dM/dt$, the change in the nominal stock of money or government debt. Consumers save a fraction of their disposable income. But how shall we define disposable income? The standard social accounting definition would start with net national product, add transfers and subtract taxes. We could follow that convention. It has the implication that households ignore their capital gains and losses when they make spending-saving decisions. That may be reasonable for short-run analysis; but in dealing with economic growth and the possibility of permanent steady inflation, it seems more sensible to include capital gains, positive or negative, in the income measure that governs the spending of households. A capital gain occurs, in this economy, when a fall in the price level increases the real value of holdings of money.

For my purposes, then, disposable income in current prices is net national product less taxes plus transfers plus capital gains on money balances. These capital gains can be valued in current prices as $-Mp'/p$; if I hold government debt with a face value of £100 and the price level falls by 3 per cent, I make a capital gain of £3. From the definition of the government deficit given a moment ago, it follows that disposable income equals $pQ + M' - hpQ - Mp'/p = (1-h)pQ + M' - Mp'/p$. Real disposable income is thus $(1-h)Q + M/p (M'/M - p'/p)$. The last term is just $d/dt (M/p)$, the absolute change in real holdings of government debt.

Households wish to save, in real terms, the fraction s of real disposable income defined in this way.

Some of this saving will take the form of additional holdings of real capital, what we usually speak of as 'investment'. But some of it will take the form of additional holdings of government debt. We will have to come back to this portfolio decision later. In the meanwhile, we can say that households will spend the fraction $1-s$ of real disposable income on real consumption. The government, we know, makes real purchases of goods and services equal to hQ. Along any full-employment path, the remainder of full-employment output will have to go into real capital formation. It follows that, along any full-employment path

$$Q = (1-s)\,\{(1-h)\,Q + \mathrm{d}/\mathrm{d}t(M/p)\} + hQ + \mathrm{d}K/\mathrm{d}t,$$

which simplifies to

$$\mathrm{d}K/\mathrm{d}t = (1-h)\,sQ - (1-s)\,\mathrm{d}/\mathrm{d}t(M/p).$$

Since we have some new concepts, we need some new notation. Let $m = M/pQ$ be the ratio of the real or nominal stock of money to the real or nominal flow of output; it is, therefore, the reciprocal of the income velocity of money. Let θ be the proportional rate of growth of the nominal money supply, a policy parameter; and let ϕ be the rate of inflation, the proportional rate of growth of the commodity price level. Remember that $v = K/Q$ is the capital/output ratio. Then with a little manipulation, the last equation becomes

$$K'/K = (1-h)\,s/v - (1-s)\,(\theta-\phi)\,m/v.$$

In a steady state, the stock of real capital must be growing at the same rate as employment in efficiency units, for only then can the capital/output ratio be constant along with all rates of growth. If the natural rate of growth is g, then in a steady state, we must have

$$g = (1-h)\,s/v - (1-s)\,(\theta-\phi)m/v.$$

If we eliminate government consumption, so $h = 0$, and

eliminate the paper asset, so $m = 0$, this reduces to $g = s/v$, the Harrod–Domar consistency condition for the non-monetary economy. What we have, therefore, is a generalized Harrod–Domar condition.

It is worth a moment to interpret this new formula, to understand how the new assumptions have changed the basic consistency condition for steady-state growth. Now s is the ratio of saving to disposable income. Even if the government always balanced its budget, the ratio of saving to net national product would be smaller than s, smaller by a factor equal to the ratio of disposable income to net national product, which would be $1 - h$. That accounts for the first term. But the government does not necessarily balance its budget. When it does not, it makes real transfers to the private economy, positive or negative according as the budget shows a deficit or a surplus. As we have seen, when account is taken of capital gains and losses on outstanding government debt, the net addition to disposable income is simply the change in the real value of the government debt, $\mathrm{d}/\mathrm{d}t\,(M/p)$.

In the equation for $\mathrm{d}K/\mathrm{d}t$, a unit change in M/p generates s units of private saving. But each unit increase in M/p is a unit increase in private wealth, and must find a home in the private economy's balance sheet, It does more than satisfy the saving that it generates; it absorbs a whole unit of saving, or it displaces a whole unit of real capital—these are pessimistic and optimistic ways of describing the same fact. This accounts for the second component of $\mathrm{d}K/\mathrm{d}t$, the term $-(1-s)\mathrm{d}/\mathrm{d}t(M/p)$.

The generalized version of the Harrod–Domar condition merely translates all this into per-unit-of-capital terms, and requires that, for a steady state to be possible, the amount of saving per unit of capital available for real net investment should be just enough to make the stock of capital grow as fast as the supply of labour in efficiency units. Then and only then can all the economic magnitudes grow at constant rates and the capital/output ratio be constant. In addition, this form of the equation makes it clear that the existence of a public debt makes a difference to private saving only if its real value is actually changing, that is, if the nominal debt is changing at a rate different from the rate at which the price level is changing.

This can not, however, be the end of the story. Three new symbols now appear in the Harrod–Domar condition (the allowance for public consumption—h—could have been included in a non-monetary model, so I do not count it). One of them, θ, the growth rate of the nominal stock of money or public debt, is a policy parameter. But the other two, ϕ, the rate of inflation, and m, the ratio of government debt to net national product, are in general economic variables. They can not simply be prescribed. The government does control the nominal amount of its outstanding debt. But if the owners of private wealth are dissatisfied with the composition of their portfolio as between real capital and money balances, they will attempt to exchange one for the other. They can not affect the asset totals for the economy as a whole, except by the long-run process of net investment. But in the course of trying to do so, even in the short run, they will bid up or bid down the price of commodities in terms of money. They can, therefore, influence the rate of inflation, and they can affect the real value of the stock of money. To complete the model, something needs to be said about the determination of ϕ and m.

An economy with a capital market can be in equilibrium only if the existing supplies of money and real capital find a welcome place in the consolidated balance sheet of the private economy. The savings decision has to be supplemented by a portfolio decision. Nothing too subtle is required here, since we are interested mainly in the qualitative properties of steady states.

It will be enough if we agree that there is a transactions demand for money and an asset demand, which need not be additive, of course. The most important determinant of the transactions demand for money is presumably the volume of transactions; but ordinary inventory theory suggests that the opportunity cost of holding money should play a role too.

Since I have already introduced the demand for money in

the form of the ratio of real cash balances to national product, it will be convenient to capture the transactions demand for money in terms of that ratio. The assumption that transactions demand is simply proportional to total output is too crude. It is more plausible, though still special, to make m a decreasing function of the opportunity cost of holding money.

Now the opportunity cost of holding money is, in this simple economy, the difference between the yield on real capital and the yield on holdings of money. The yield on real capital is what is variously called the rate of profit, or the own-rate of return, or the net rental per pound's worth of capital. I shall call this rate of return r. It need not equal the marginal product of the capital good, as it would if all markets were perfectly competitive. But I will assume that the rate of return is higher the higher is employment per unit of capital or, equivalently, the higher is output per unit of capital, or the lower is the capital/output ratio. That is an assumption I have made before, in order to allow for different propensities to save wages and profits. It seems natural enough in the long-run context.

If we think of the paper asset as ordinary currency, i.e. non-interest-bearing government debt, then the yield on money balances is the negative of the rate of inflation, $-\phi$. If the price level falls by 1 per cent, the owner of currency receives a return of 1 per cent; if the price level rises by 1 per cent, the owner of cash receives a return of -1 per cent. If the paper asset is a short-term government bond, bearing the nominal interest rate of $100i$ per cent, then the yield on it is $i-\phi$, which is just Fisher's real rate of interest.

There are obvious practical difficulties in the way of paying interest in a circulating medium of exchange. The accurate thing to do would be to set up a three-asset model in which the government issued a zero-interest debt that served as medium of exchange and an interest-bearing debt that did not. The first would satisfy a transactions demand and the second would not. But that would involve me in complications: there would have to be a more detailed set of portfolio preferences for capitalists and a debt-management policy for government. Instead, I will try to have the best of both worlds at the cost of some strain on the imagination by assuming that the government does pay a nominal interest rate on its debt, while I continue to call the debt money and suppose that it does serve as the medium of exchange. This peculiar device will in the end serve to say something about reality. I hope it will not be obtrusive, because I will seldom need to imagine changing the nominal interest rate.

The opportunity cost of holding money is, therefore, $r-(i-\phi) = r-i+\phi$, the difference between the return on real capital and the return on government debt. (You may notice that I could have interpreted a rise in the price level as a capital gain for owners of real capital instead of a capital loss for owners of money; then the yield on real capital would have been $r+\phi$ and the return on government debt simply i. The difference would still be $r-i+\phi$.)

I have suggested that the transactions demand for money will depend in part on this opportunity cost or yield differential. The same yield differential will presumably be a major determinant of the asset demand for money, operating in the same way. The higher is the yield on real capital relative to the yield on money, that is to say, the higher is $r-i+\phi$, the smaller should be the desired stock of real balances for any given level of output, i.e. the smaller should be the desired value of m. In addition, the notion of portfolio balance may suggest that the capital/output ratio itself be entered as an independent determinant of the demand for money. For given total income and asset yields, the demand for each asset presumably depends on aggregate private wealth. This dependence can be allowed for by making m, the ratio of monetary wealth to income, an increasing function of v, the ratio of capital to income.

If I write

$$m = m\,(v, r-i+\phi)$$

the partial derivative of m with respect to v will be positive—with a given volume of transactions to accommodate and with given yields, a community that owns more real capital will wish to own more government debt. The partial derivative of m with respect to its second argument will be negative—other things equal, a higher rate of profit on real capital, or a lower rate of interest on government debt, or a higher rate of inflation reduces the demand for government debt per unit of output. Finally, from the definition of m, with a given capital/output ratio and given yields on all assets, the nominal demand for money is proportional to the current value of aggregate output.

In this demand function for government debt, r is certainly not an independent parameter. In fact, I have already assumed that r is a decreasing function of v. For given i and ϕ, therefore, the total derivative of m with respect to v is positive; m is an increasing function of v. Indeed, for very small v the economy has very little capital per unit of output, and real capital earns a relatively high return; for both reasons it is reasonable to presume that m will be very small, perhaps not far from zero, as v tends towards zero.

We can now return to the discussion of steady states. In a monetary economy, it is natural to amend the definition of a steady state to require a constant rate of inflation; since everything else is growing exponentially, the price level ought to be no exception. In any steady state, the Harrod–Domar condition has to be satisfied, and in addition the portfolio-balance equation must also be satisfied. We thus have two equations:

$$m = m\ (v, r-i+\phi),$$
$$g = (1-h)\ s/v - (1-s)\ (\theta-\phi)m/v.$$

Since v is constant in a steady state, r is constant. So is i and so is ϕ. It follows from the portfolio-balance equation that m is constant in a steady state; the nominal stock of money must be growing at the same rate as the value of output in current prices. But real output is growing at the natural rate g and the price level is rising at the rate ϕ (which may be negative). Therefore $\theta = \phi+g$ and $\theta-\phi = g$. In more commonplace terms we can say: in a steady state, with all asset yields constant, the income velocity of money will be constant; therefore the price level will rise at a rate equal to the excess of the rate of growth of the money supply over the rate of growth of real output. We can substitute this result into the Harrod–Domar condition and solve it for m, to get

$$m = (1-h)s/(1-s)g - v/(1-s).$$

In the $m-v$ plane, this is the equation of a downward-sloping straight line (see Figure 8). Any point on it satisfies

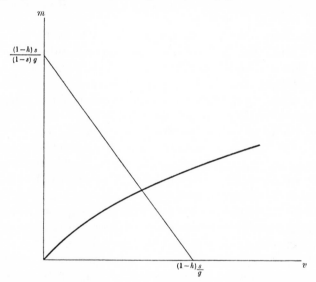

FIG. 8. Portfolio-balance curve and Harrod–Domar locus in a two-asset model

the Harrod–Domar condition. An economy with a large supply of government debt corresponds to a low capital/output ratio because the large budget deficits that give rise to the debt are an offset to private saving; the issue of government debt displaces real capital from the portfolio of the private economy. Notice that as m becomes small, the steady state v tends to $(1-h)s/g$, which is the Harrod–Domar value in a non-monetary economy.

Although any point on the line satisfies the Harrod–Domar condition, the fiscal-monetary policy of the government selects a particular point consistent with the portfolio preferences of the private economy. To see this, replace ϕ by $\theta - g$ in the portfolio-balance equation so that it reads:

$$m = m(v,\, r-i+\theta-g).$$

Here g is a constant of nature and i and θ are policy parameters. Once they are fixed by the government, we have another equation in m and v that can be drawn on the same diagram; I have already argued that it starts at or near the origin and has a positive slope.

The restrictions I have placed on the portfolio-balance curve ensure that the two curves will intersect once and only once. The horizontal coordinate of the intersection gives the capital/output ratio in the unique steady state compatible with portfolio equilibrium. And knowledge of the capital/output ratio unlocks all the rest of the facts about the steady state. For example, in the steady state, disposable income is $(1-h)Q+gM/p$, so consumption per unit of capital is $(1-s)\{(1-h)/v+mg/v\} = (1-s)(1-h+mg)/v$. On the other hand, we know that output per unit of capital, $1/v$, is in one-to-one correspondence with employment per unit of capital, so the latter is known as well. Consumption per head is just the ratio of consumption per unit of capital to employment per unit of capital. Provided only that a wide enough range of capital/output ratios is actually achievable, each set of natural and policy parameters corresponds to a steady state.

THE NEUTRALITY OF MONEY IN A GROWING ECONOMY

We can now answer the question about the neutrality of money in this growing economy. Suppose the government sets a higher value of θ; it runs bigger deficits and causes the supply of government debt to grow at a faster rate. Suppose also that the economy reaches a new steady state, though that is a gratuitous assumption at this stage of the game.

How will the new steady state differ from the old? The rate of inflation will be higher, just as much higher than the old rate as the new θ is higher than the old θ, because $\phi = \theta - g$. Is that all?

The line in the $m - v$ plane showing points where the Harrod–Domar condition is satisfied is independent of θ, so it does not shift. But the portfolio-balance curve does shift. A higher rate of inflation increases the opportunity cost of holding money; it therefore reduces the real demand for money corresponding to each value of v. The portfolio-balance curve rotates downward in the diagram. The new steady state has a higher capital/output ratio (and a lower ratio of money supply to national product) than the old. There is a superficial paradox here: a more rapid increase in the nominal money supply moves the economy nearer to the state of affairs that would rule in a non-monetary economy. It does so because the flight from money set off by the higher rate of inflation will generate a price level high enough to reduce the ratio of cash balances to money income.

It appears, then, that money is not neutral in a growing economy, at least not in this very long-run sense: the real characteristics of the steady state depend on the rate of monetary growth. One can see why. Remember, first of all, that money is created in this economy not by open-market operations but by government budget deficits. So every increase in the money supply is an increase in private wealth, at least in nominal terms. This increase can be neutralized in real terms by a correspondingly rapid rise in the price level. But if the price level rises faster, with the nominal interest rate constant, the result is a one-for-one fall in the real rate of interest. This is the route by which variations in the rate of monetary growth manage to have real effects. A government that wishes merely to have a different rate of inflation, without any corresponding change in the steady-state capital/output ratio or anything else, can do so in this model by changing θ and i in parallel. That will leave the portfolio-balance curve where it was, and the combined change will be neutral so far as the real economy is concerned.

There is one other thing to be said on this question of neutrality. The point in the diagram corresponding to a non-monetary economy, one that has no asset alternative to real capital, is the intersection of the Harrod–Domar line with the horizontal axis. Evidently the non-monetary economy will have a higher capital/output ratio than a monetary economy with the same technology and the same saving rate out of disposable income.

NON-STEADY-STATE PATHS WITH TWO ASSETS

So far I have discussed only the steady-state properties of a monetary economy. In earlier lectures I have also analysed full-employment paths that were not themselves steady states. The typical conclusion was always that all full-employment paths with constant saving rates eventually transformed themselves into steady states whatever their starting points. Does the existence of a monetary asset make any difference to this result? The answer is that it does. The study of the non-steady-state behaviour of a monetary economy raises questions more difficult than any we have seen so far. They have only begun to be studied in the literature and there is still a lot to be found out. The most I can hope to do is give you some idea of what the problems are and how they arise.

The difficulty arises because we have so far had very little to say about another economic variable that enters the model, the rate of inflation. It was not hard to agree that in a steady state the rate of inflation must be constant, and must actually be equal to the difference between the rate of growth of the money supply and the natural rate of growth of aggregate output. Once we leave the steady state, no such simple rule will do. Indeed, once we leave the steady state the question arises whether the portfolio-balance equation is satisfied at every moment of time. If it is, if the money market is always in equilibrium, then that determines the rate of inflation. The portfolio-balance equation says that $m = m(v, r(v)$ $-i+\phi)$. Everything in this equation is given in the short run except for ϕ: the stock of money is given by past fiscal-monetary decisions; the level of output is given by past capital accumulation, the supply of labour, and the full-employment rule; the capital/output ratio is given because both the stock of capital and the level of output are given; and the nominal rate of interest is given as a policy decision. If portfolio balance rules, the current rate of inflation must be the equilibrating variable. The price level must rise just fast enough or just slow enough to induce private owners of wealth to hold the existing stocks of money and capital.

This approach can be improved upon by supposing the portfolio-balance equation to hold in terms of an expected rate of inflation, not the actual current rate of inflation. There must then be another mechanism to show how the expected rate of inflation is generated out of past actual rates of inflation. The advantage of this finesse is that one can study how the behaviour of the economy depends on the volatility of expectations and, as you might expect in an inflationary situation, that dependence can be very important.

Alternatively, one could give up the notion that the money market is in equilibrium all the time, and make the rate of inflation depend on the excess demand or supply in the market for government debt. But then, by Walras' Law, at least one of the commodity markets must be out of equilibium too. Eventually that particular nut will have to be cracked; but this is no time to open up all the further problems that I have so far swept aside by the assumption of maintained full employment.

Suppose that the money market *is* always in equilibrium; and suppose further that we could afford to ignore variations in the rate of inflation from its steady-state value $\theta - g$. I do not claim that we *can* afford to ignore the changing rate of inflation; indeed I want to show that that is the nub of the problem. If we could fix the rate of inflation that way, in the confidence that any variations were negligibly small, then we could easily show that any full-employment path tends to the steady state corresponding to the values of the policy variables θ and i.

We already know from the discussion of saving behaviour and the full employment rule that

$$K'/K = (1-h)s/v - (1-s)(\theta - \phi)m/v.$$

Employment in efficiency units is always growing at the rate g. Since output per unit of capital is an increasing function of employment per unit of capital, output per unit of capital will rise or fall according as employment in efficiency units rises or falls faster than the stock of capital. In other words, the capital/output ratio, v, will rise or fall according as K'/K is greater or less than g, i.e. according as $(1-h)s/v - (1-s)(\theta - \phi)m/v$ is greater or less than g. Provided that the rate of inflation is very nearly constant, so $\theta - \phi$ is

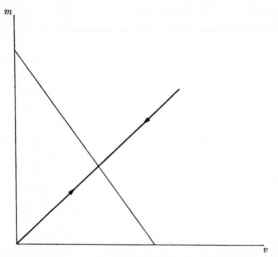

FIG. 9. Approach to steady state with perpetual portfolio balance

approximately equal to g; this amounts to saying that v increases everywhere to the left of the Harrod–Domar locus in Figure 9, and decreases everywhere to the right of it.

If the portfolio-balance equation holds all the time, with $\theta - \phi$ near g, the economy—characterized by its m and v—must always be on or at least very near the upward-sloping curve in the diagram, for that curve is precisely the graph of $m = m(v, r-i+\theta-g)$. If the economy is confined to that curve, and v moves as I have just described, then it is plain that the economy must travel along the portfolio-balance curve until it intersects the Harrod–Domar curve, until the steady state is reached. In this case the story of a monetary economy is very much like the story of the one-asset economy; once the government chooses a portfolio-balance curve, by selecting a nominal interest rate and budgetary policy, the story becomes one-dimensional and every full employment path tends to the steady state.

But of course I have made the story one-dimensional by an illegitimate assumption. I assumed the money market to be always in equilibrium, with a constant rate of inflation. In general, however, outside steady states, it requires a changing rate of inflation to keep the money market in equilibrium. The demand for money will change as the capital/output ratio changes, unless there are compensating changes in the opportunity cost of holding money. There are in fact two differential equations, not one, and the story is essentially two-dimensional. I will not work out the complete analysis, though it has been done in several versions. But I will try to suggest some of the possible outcomes.

Imagine that the economy has been proceeding along a convergent path like the one I have just described, with a steady rate of inflation. Then suppose there occurs, for some unforeseen reason, a sudden change in the rate of inflation, say a decrease, for definiteness. Slower inflation means a reduction in the opportunity cost of holding money; the portfolio-balance curve rotates upward. To maintain money-market equilibrium, there must be an increase in the ratio of money supply to value of output. The normal way for this to come about is that individuals attempt to increase their own holdings of money or government debt by selling off commodities (in the form of real capital). The economy as a whole can change neither its stock of money nor its stock of capital (in the short run). But the excess demand for money (excess supply of goods) can deflate the price level and restore money-market equilibrium by reducing the money value of output.

The trouble is, as every schoolboy knows, that this process constitutes a further reduction in the rate of inflation, and it will therefore rotate the portfolio-balance curve further upward (see Figure 10), recreating a momentary disequilibrium that has to be wiped out by further deflation.

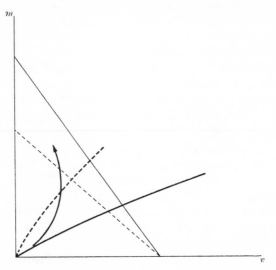

FIG. 10. Possible instability in a two-asset model

So the economy, once disturbed from its peaceful approach to the steady state, may be involved in a cumulative accelerating deflation.

During all this time the capital/output ratio has been increasing, say, if the process started to the left of the Harrod–Domar locus. But that locus, too, was drawn as of a constant rate of inflation equal to $\theta - g$. With the rate of inflation falling, the Harrod–Domar locus shifts too. In fact, it is easy to see that the horizontal intercept of the Harrod–Domar locus is unaffected by a change in the rate of inflation, so the line rotates to the left around that point when the rate of inflation falls. It is perfectly possible that at some point the

trajectory of the economy should cross the shifting Harrod–
Domar curve and come up on its other side. In that case, the
capital/output ratio, which had been increasing, begins to
decrease. In the story I have been telling, this is a stabilizing
factor; it reduces the demand for money (along the curve,
not by shifting it) both for diversification reasons and because,
by increasing the rate of profit on capital, it increases the
opportunity cost of money balances. But there is no necessity
that this stabilizing factor will be enough, and the economy
may continue in a deflationary flight to money with falling
capital/output ratio and falling output per head.

There is obviously a symmetric story to be told in which
the economy gets into a hyperinflationary situation, with
each increase in the rate of inflation requiring a reduction in
the ratio of cash balances to output, but with the resulting
flight from money speeding up the inflation and re-creating
the disequilibrium. You can think through the details for
yourself.

I suppose it is not so surprising that many-asset economies
can get into these unstable spirals; they have some of the
characteristics of speculative booms, because the demand
for something—money or real assets—depends on the associated capital gains and losses, and therefore on the *rate of
change* of a price rather than the price itself. So the increase
of a price makes an asset more attractive and drives its price
up further. The same sort of situation arises in non-monetary
models of economic growth with many different real capital
goods; it is the multiplicity of assets that makes the difference.

Why, then, do we not observe more hyperinflations or
hyperdeflations moving away from steady states? Well, one
reason, no doubt, is that governments do not simply fix a
fiscal-monetary policy once and for all and then stand back
and let it rip. But that is unlikely to be the whole reason.
Anyone who has worked at economic policy knows that the
economy does not feel as unstable as this picture suggests it
to be (even without fluctuations in employment). There is an
important analytical reason why the kind of model I have
described errs on the side of instability.

It is asking for trouble to expect the currently experienced rate of inflation to maintain perpetual portfolio balance. Suppose, instead, as I suggested earlier, that it is an 'expected' rate of inflation that appears in the portfolio-balance equation, and that the expected rate of inflation is some sort of average of past rates of inflation. That will certainly introduce an element of sluggishness into the economy. A sudden change in the rate of inflation will generate only a small immediate change in the expected rate of inflation and therefore only a small shift in the portfolio-balance curve. Disturbance is less likely to cumulate.

In fact, it has been found that there is *always* a degree of sluggishness of expectations sufficient to stabilize a monetary economy of the general sort I have described. Then once again all full-employment paths approach a steady state, but there is a different steady state for each choice of fiscal-monetary policy. It is hard to know if the required degree of sluggishness of expectations is reasonable or realistic. If it is, it might be said to turn this model from a work of fiction into a work of friction.

5

Economic Policy in a Growth Model

ANY theory that says something about the real world is likely to have implications for policy. But it is only good sense to realize that an abstract theory, like the one I have been developing, can only say abstract things about economic policy. At the very beginning, I described the aggregative theory of growth as a parable. You expect a parable to have a moral, but hardly to contain concrete instructions for the conduct of life. So here, when I talk about policy implications, I have to stay at roughly the same level of abstraction as the theory on which they are based.

There are two aspects of economic policy about which the theory, in the exposition I have given, says nothing at all. In the first place, you may have noticed that the theory has very little so say about the long-run rate of growth itself. Unless it behaves very peculiarly, the kind of economy I have been describing eventually settles down to growth at its natural rate. The natural rate of growth in the simplest case—where there is a steady state—is the sum of the rate of growth of the labour supply and the rate of purely labour-augmenting technical progress. To change the rate of growth of real output per head you have to change the rate of technical progress. That can be an object of policy, and there is now a certain amount of talk about the allocation of resources to research and development, with that end in view. But very little is known about the exact connection between research expenditure and actual technological progress as it enters models of production. In any case, policy measures of that kind involve considerations quite outside the model we have been discussing, so the model can have very little to say about them.

One of the contributions of the modern theory of growth
has been to put a damper on loose discussion of policy direc-
ted to changing the rate of growth. The year-to-year growth
of real output in an economy has three elements. Some of it
comes from year-to-year changes in the degree of utilization
or slack in the economy, as measured by the unemployment
rate or the rate of capacity utilization. An economy can grow
faster or slower from one year to the next because its unemployment rate is falling or rising. If this is to be described
as growth, it is specifically growth of demand, not growth
of supply. The growth of supply, or productive capacity, has
two further components. One is the underlying steady-state
rate of growth, the natural rate, the other is the growth that
comes from a current or recent change in the proportion of
output invested. The theory says that this last component
of growth is transitory; it depends on investing an increasing
share of output, not on investing a high share of output. A
rate of growth higher than the natural rate can be maintained
for ever only by a steady increase in the investment quota,
eventually to 100 per cent and beyond, if donors can be
found. (It is only fair to add, however, that the stimulus
from a once-for-all jump in the investment quota may last
for some time. For how long a time depends on the empirical
characteristics of the technology, including the sort of re-
finement I discussed in the third chapter.) When we talk
about changing the economy's rate of growth, it is useful to
keep straight which components we have in mind.

I have so far been neglecting the very first component of
growth—changes in the utilization of productive capacity—
by holding to the assumption of continuous full employment,
or at least a constant unemployment rate. I am going to
continue to do so. The government of the model economy
I described last week had, in principle, two policy tools, a
fiscal policy and a monetary policy. (They were mixed up in
that model, but a more complete description would allow
fiscal policy to control the outstanding volume of public
debt and monetary policy to control the composition of the
outstanding debt as between the monetized portion and

the non-monetized portion.) Every real government, with a complicated system of taxes, subsidies, objects of expenditure, and direct controls, would have more than two policy tools. I shall assume that the government uses one, or some, of them to maintain a steady, or fairly steady, rate of unemployment. That is the second branch of economic policy that the theory says nothing particular about.

Does that leave anything for the government of our model economy to do? There are, in fact, two remaining objects of policy. The society can decide, on grounds to be discussed, which of the possible steady states it would like the economy ultimately to be in. And then it can decide how, and at what pace, it would like to get there from here. That formulation appears to beg a question: how do we know that the best path for the economy to follow might not be one that does not approach a steady state? Perhaps the best path has a saving rate that changes enough, and often enough, to keep the economy away from any steady state. The answer is that the full analysis of an optimal path for the economy, which I shall not try to give, shows that the optimal saving rate, while it is not constant at the beginning, does always move toward a best constant value, so that the economy does move toward a best steady state.

A WELFARE FUNCTION FOR GROWTH PATHS

I am going to proceed on the assumption that the desirability of a path depends only on the consumption that it gives at every instant of time. Therefore, to steer the economy, the government need only control the allocation of output between consumption and investment. (In a more detailed model, it would have to look after the allocation of investment between the consumption-goods industry and the capital-goods industry.) It is simplest to imagine that the government makes the allocation decision directly, as if the economy were centrally planned, and that is what I shall do. But the government of the simple monetary economy I dealt with last time could accomplish the same thing indirectly, provided it had a policy tool left over after maintaining full employment. It would have to manœuvre its fiscal-monetary policy so that, given the saving rate from disposable income, and taking account of the absorption of private saving by increases in the public debt, it induces the public to consume just the amount that they should along the optimal path. Easier said than done, no doubt; but what isn't?

Whatever device it uses, the government of this model economy must pick out the capital/output ratio v^* that it eventually wants to reach; then it must steer the economy towards a steady state with that capital/output ratio. Suppose that the target state of affairs is one with considerably more capital per head (in efficiency units) than the initial state of affairs—that is presumably the realistic situation. There are draconian paths that reduce consumption drastically, invest rapidly, and reach the target relatively quickly. These are paths of fast initial growth. There are more indulgent paths that keep consumption fairly high in the early stages, accumulate capital more slowly, and reach the target after a longer time. These are paths of slower initial growth. The two questions we have to answer are: how is the target to be chosen, and how does one weigh the advantages of the draconian and indulgent approach paths?

Any explicit answer to these questions must be based on an explicit criterion for comparing the social value of alternative paths: a social welfare function for this kind of problem. I have already stipulated that the value of a path depends only on the consumption stream associated with it; so we need a way of comparing or ordering consumption streams. There is actually only one way of doing this that has led to any useful results at all. First, we define an instantaneous utility function for society. Let $C(t)$ stand for aggregate consumption at time t and $L(t)$ for aggregate employment or population (in natural units, not efficiency units, even if there is labour-augmenting technical progress) at time t. Then the instantaneous utility generated at time is a function of consumption per head, multiplied by the number of heads: it is $LU(C/L)$, where U is a conventional utility function, with positive but diminishing marginal utility. Now the social value of a consumption stream is calculated by discounting each instantaneous utility back to the present by some rate of social time preference, and adding up (integrating) the discounted utilities over the whole future. In formal terms, the criterion is

$$\int_0^\infty e^{-at} L U(C/L) \mathrm{d}t \; = \; L_0 \int_0^\infty e^{-(a-n)t} U(c) \mathrm{d}t,$$

where a is the rate of social time preference, n is the rate of growth of population, and c is consumption per head.

There is no good way to escape the valuation of infinite consumption streams, no matter how unattractive the idea is. Planning for a finite horizon must involve placing a value on capital left over at the end of the planning period, because otherwise an optimizing plan will consume all capital in its last years—why shouldn't it? But there is no rational way to value terminal capital except by implicit or explicit consideration of what happens after the planning period is over. But then, better explicit than implicit. The fact that the planning horizon is infinite creates mathematical difficulties; the social-welfare integrals may not exist. There are refinements that cover some (but not all) of those difficult cases; but I shall stick to the cases where the rate of time preference is large enough compared with the rate of population growth, so that the integrals are well behaved.

One other aspect of this welfare criterion calls for comment. It makes consumption at different time periods independent goods in the sense that the marginal contribution to social welfare from an increment to consumption at time t depends only on how much consumption was already scheduled for time t, and not at all on the consumption scheduled at other times. You could say that this scheme fails to penalize irregular consumption paths, though most societies would seem to prefer smoothly increasing consumption paths to irregular and occasionally decreasing consumption paths. That is so; but it turns out that optimal paths under this criterion usually do show smoothly increasing consumption, so that the criticism is probably not important.

A NECESSARY CONDITION FOR OPTIMALITY

The formal problem facing a planning board or government that has just taken office at time 0 is to maximize

$$W = \int_0^\infty e^{-(a-n)t} U(c) \mathrm{d}t.$$

It is allowed to choose any feasible path for consumption per head. The economy starts with a historically given stock of capital and a given supply of labour, and therefore with a given productive capacity. It consumes a certain amount of its initial output and accumulates the rest. But this decision determines how much capital it will have an instant later and therefore how much productive capacity, since labour supply and technology are exogenously given. Once again an allocation decision is made, and a still later capital stock is determined. The planning board can choose any consumption path that does not ever involve it in any physical impossibility, like a negative capital stock or negative gross investment.

Mathematically speaking, this is a problem in the calculus or variations. It was first tackled by Frank Ramsey as long ago as 1928, with the simplifying assumptions of constant population and stationary technology. Now, with the development of the modern theory of growth, more complicated versions of the problem are being studied with more powerful tools. I shall limit myself to an intuitive—but fairly rigorous—deduction of a basic necessary condition satisfied by any optimal path. It will tell us most of what we need to know.

Suppose the planning board has found an optimal path $c^*(t)$. (To be quite honest, I have to suppose that this path does not verge on any of the impossibilities mentioned earlier.) Then it has to be the case that any infinitesimally small variation around the path c^* leaves the welfare integral stationary; because if it increased the welfare integral, the variation would be worth making and c^* could not be optimal, while if altering the plan slightly caused the welfare

integral to decrease there would be a symmetric variation with all signs changed that would increase welfare and again c^* could not be optimal.

I want to apply this idea—which you may recognize as the fundamental argument in all maximization problems—to a particular test variation around the optimal oath. Follow c^* until some arbitrary time t; then for a very short interval save a very little extra over and above what was saved on the c^* path. The result will be that at time $t+h$, say, the capital stock will be a bit bigger than along the c^* path; keep it exactly that much bigger for the rest of time; consume whatever extra net output the extra capital yields. If c^* is optimal, this variation must leave the welfare integral unchanged.

The change in the welfare integral consists of a one-time sacrifice of consumption at time t and a perpetual gain in consumption after time t. For the welfare integral to be stationary, the sacrifice and the gain must just cancel. A reduction of, say, one unit in total consumption at time t amounts to a reduction of e^{-nt} units in consumption per head, and therefore to a reduction of $e^{nt}U'\{c^*(t)\}e^{-nt}$ or just $U'\{c(t)\}$ in the instantaneous social utility at time t. The present value of this change at time 0 is $e^{-at}U'(c^*)$.

Now we must calculate the value of the perpetual gain. The sacrifice of one unit of consumption for, say, one unit of time will yield one extra unit of capital. The test-path maintains the stock of capital forever one unit higher than it was on the path giving c^*. Let $r^*(s)$ be the net marginal product of capital at time s on the optimal path. Then at every time s, from t onward, the test path can give an extra $r^*(s)$ of aggregate consumption. That amounts to an increment of $e^{-ns}r^*(s)$ in consumption per head at time s, and therefore to an increment in instantaneous social utility equal to $e^{ns}U'\{c^*(s)\}e^{-ns}r^*(s) = U'\{c^*(s)\}r^*(s)$. To calculate the whole gain in social welfare, we must discount this quantity back to time zero and then integrate the result from t onward. The total gain is therefore $\int_{t}^{\infty} e^{-as}r^*(s)U'\{c^*(s)\}\mathrm{d}s$. If c^* is in fact an optimal path, it is necessary that

$$e^{-at}U'\{c^*(t)\} = \int_t^\infty e^{-as}r^*(s)U'\{c^*(s)\}ds.$$

This condition must hold for every t, because t was an arbitrary moment of time in the construction of the alternative test-path. It is permissible, therefore, to differentiate this equation with respect to t. The result is

$$-ae^{-at}U'+e^{-at}d/dt(U') = -e^{-at}r^*(t)U'\{c^*(t)\},$$

which reduces to

$$\frac{d/dt(U')}{U'} = -\{r^*(t)-a\}$$

In words, this condition says that an optimal path must have the property that at every time the social marginal utility of consumption per head must be falling at a rate equal to the excess of the marginal product of capital over the rate of time preference.

PROPERTIES OF THE OPTIMAL PATH

This condition implies one natural property of an optimal path: so long as the marginal product of capital exceeds the rate of time preference, the marginal utility of consumption per head must be falling, and so consumption per head must be rising. If that is to keep happening, capital per head must be rising, so investment must be going on, and the capital/output ratio rising. But the important thing about this condition is that it comes very close to defining a complete strategy for the planning board.

At each moment of time, the existing capital stock is known, and so is the supply of labour (the volume of employment, since full employment is being maintained). Therefore the marginal product of capital is known. The planning board also knows what consumption per head was a moment ago. It must compare the marginal product of capital with the rate of time preference, and choose the current level of consumption just high enough so that the proportional fall in the marginal utility of consumption per head is equal to r^*-a. This amount of consumption, substracted from the total net output producible by the existing capital and labour, leaves current net investment. Therefore an instant from now the planning board will know the stock of capital and can perform the whole operation again.

The only thing lacking for a complete solution to the problem is the initial consumption at time zero. The planning board inherits a capital stock at time zero, but it can choose initial consumption—though not according to the rule just given, for that requires knowledge of *optimal* consumption a moment ago.

There is one and only one correct choice of initial consumption. The planning board will find that if it chooses any other initial consumption and then applies the rule for ever after, it will get into trouble. If it chooses initial consumption too low, it will find that the rule eventually tells it to accumulate capital like mad and reduce consumption towards zero in an obviously non-optimal way. If the board chooses initial consumption too high, the rule will eventually tell it to let the economy's capital stock run down to zero in finite time. Neither prospect should appeal to reasonable chaps. In between is a value for initial consumption that avoids both troubles when the optimal strategy is followed. That is the correct starting point, and the whole problem is solved.

This optimal path approaches a steady state. It would take too long to give a detailed argument for this proposition, but I can make it plausible. For this purpose, carry out the differentiation in the last equation to get

$$\frac{U''(c^*)\mathrm{d}c^*/\mathrm{d}t}{U'(c^*)} = \frac{c^*U''(c^*)}{U'(c^*)}\frac{1}{c^*}\frac{\mathrm{d}c^*}{\mathrm{d}t} = -j\frac{(c^*)'}{c^*} = -(r^*-a).$$

Here j is minus the elasticity of the marginal instantaneous social utility of consumption per head; it is a positive number because of diminishing marginal utility. From now on, I will suppose j to be a constant; that is, I specialize to a constant-elasticity instantaneous social utility function. The larger j is, the more sharply the marginal social utility of consumption falls, and therefore the more the planning board is likely to favour poor people—ourselves—against rich people —our descendants. That is now visible from the formula, which states that $c^{*\prime}/c^* = (r^*-a)/j$. Supposing, as is normal, that the marginal productivity of capital exceeds the rate of time preference, so that capital is being accumulated and therefore consumption per head is growing, the higher is j the slower will be the optimal rate of growth of consumption per head. This means that high j is associated with low investment per head and therefore with high current consumption. The optimal rate of growth of consumption per head at any time is compounded out of the current state of technology and considerations of intergenerational equity, in this rather simple way. In this form, the formula gives clear instructions to the planning board.

Now I want to argue heuristically that the optimal rate of growth of consumption per head must tend to a constant; and the only possible constant is the natural rate of growth of output per head, the rate of labour-augmenting technical progress. I cannot quite do that. But I can point out that if consumption grows at a faster rate than the natural rate of growth, the capital stock must do the same; otherwise consumption would grow faster than output and eventually absorb it all. But if the capital stock grows faster than the natural rate (the sum of the rates of growth of employment and technology), the marginal product of capital must fall steadily. From the optimality formula, that will decrease the rate of growth of consumption per head and will eventually choke it off altogether. But then the same argument can be made in reverse: growth of consumption more slowly than the natural rate of growth must either mean non-optimality or a very high level of current consumption. In the latter case investment is small, the capital stock grows slowly, the marginal product of capital rises, and the rate of growth of consumption increases. This line of argument does show that consumption cannot grow permanently at a rate faster or slower than the natural rate. It would take more mathematics than I want to do to rule out the possibility of perpetual oscillation of the optimal rate of growth, above and below the natural rate. But it is ruled out: the optimal path moves towards a situation in which consumption and output are growing at the natural rate. The ratio of real investment to output is therefore eventually constant. If follows from what we know of such models that the optimal path tends to a steady state, namely the one corresponding to the constant saving rate that eventually gets established.

We can say more about the 'best' steady state. Let $g-n = f$, the rate of labour-augmenting technical progress, which is, as we know, the steady-state rate of growth of output and consumption per head. Then in the best steady state, we must have $r^* = a+jf$. The marginal product of capital must be constant and exceed the 'pure' rate of time preference by an amount that allows for the diminishing marginal utility of consumption that goes with increasing consumption per head. In fact $a+jf$ is the number that plays the part of the equilibrium rate of interest in the best steady state; it is the rate at which commodity flows are to be discounted (while a is the rate at which instantaneous utility flows are discounted).

If we know the aggregate production function (which I have used mainly as a relation between output per unit of capital and employment per unit of capital), we can pass from the best steady-state value of r to the best steady-state value of v. Along that function, provided the one-capital-good assumption doesn't lead to serious error, each marginal product of capital will correspond to one average product of capital or one capital/output ratio. But then the Harrod–Domar condition will tell us what saving rate leads to the best v^* or steady-state capital/output ratio.

AN EXAMPLE

I illustrate with the case of a Cobb–Douglas aggregate production function, usually the easiest one to deal with.

(Remember, there are constant returns to scale and labour-augmenting technical progress.) The Cobb–Douglas function is characterized by its constant elasticity of output with respect to capital, which I shall call b. But b is the ratio of the marginal product to the average product of capital. Therefore always $b = rv$ along a Cobb–Douglas production function. We know that the optimal steady-state $r^* = a + jf$. It follows that the best steady-state capital/output ratio is $v^* = b/(a+jf)$. Moreover, in any steady state the Harrod–Domar consistency condition holds, so that always $s = gv$, where $g = n+f$ is the natural rate of growth of output. The best choice for the ultimate saving rate, constant once the optimal steady state is reached, is $s^* = gv^* = gb/(a+jf)$. It is, you can see, a function of all the parameters of the model.

It is interesting to ask whether this line of thought leads to high or low saving-rates. Obviously not much can be said in general without some guesses at appropriate values for the parameters. The only general statement one can make is that s^* is less than b. This comes from the observation that the infinite social welfare integral will not converge if $a+jf$ is less than g. If this solution makes any sense at all, then, the optimal steady-state saving rate must be less than the elasticity of aggregate output with respect to capital. If we take the usual estimates seriously, that tells us only that s^* is less than about $1/4$. Since s is to be interpreted as the ratio of net investment to net national product, that is not telling us much.

It does tell us, however, that the optimal steady state is not the steady state with the highest maintainable consumption per head. I discussed that problem briefly earlier in this book, and showed that the steady state with the highest possible consumption per head was the one in which net investment was always equal to the total of competitively-imputed profits, or the investment quota just equal to the competitively-imputed share of profits in net output. For the Cobb–Douglas case, then, steady-state consumption per head is maximized when the saving rate is set equal to b. Why does the optimal steady state save less than that? If the society I have been describing were to find itself in that position, it would want to redistribute income from the future to the present—that is, to reduce its savings—for two reasons: because it has time preference, i.e. values current utility more than future utility, and because it has diminishing marginal utility, i.e. would wish to transfer consumption from the rich future to the poorer present.

Obviously, one would not want to take simple formulas from simple models with deadly seriousness, though I am not absolutely certain they are worse than vague pontification based on unspecified assumptions. But even a simple formula can give some indication of how the best long-run saving rate depends on characteristics of the technology and of social preferences. This formula contains few surprises. For instance, a faster rate of population growth goes along with a higher saving-rate; because if the saving rate were unchanged the larger posterity would be relatively worse off, and if the situation were just right before the change, society would want to offset part of the deterioration.

The higher the rate of social time preference, the lower the optimal saving-rate; that result needs no comment.

It is rather more interesting to ask whether a faster rate of technological progress goes along with a higher or lower optimal saving-rate. The answer is that it depends on the sign of $a-nj$. If a is greater than nj, then faster technical progress should mean a higher saving rate; if a is less than nj, it should mean the reverse. Other things equal, a society with a very high rate of time preference should save more if technical progress speeds up; a society with very equalitarian tastes (a high value of j) should save less. There must be a clear intuitive reason for this result, but I haven't found it. (It is worth a reminder that not all parameter values are possible in this theory. I have already mentioned that the welfare integral will not converge if $a+jf$ is less than $n+f$, so this inequality must be respected. It is broad enough to allow a to be either greater or less than nj.)

Despite what I said about not taking simple formulas seriously, it is irresistible to find out what sort of saving rates are implied by the optimality formula. For that one has to take a stab at each of the parameters. Suppose $b = 0.25$, $n = 0.01$, so population is growing at 1 per cent a year, and $f = 0.03$, so the natural rate of growth of aggregate output is 4 per cent a year. The social-preference parameters are much more difficult, of course. One has to get a grip on what they mean. To take $a = 0.02$ is to say that if consumption per head were the same 36 years from now as it is today, you would value the consumption of your children and grand-children then half as much as you value your own consumption now. To take $a = 0.01$ is to value it at 70 per cent of your own. People differ; Frank Ramsey, who started this theory—and died young—thought that time preference was a human failing or a reflection of human mortality, so that society, which intends to live for ever, should put $a = 0$. Society is less certain nowadays of living for ever. Perhaps $0.01-0.02$ is the right range for a.

I have remarked that a high value of j makes the marginal social utility of consumption per head fall sharply, so a high j corresponds to equalitarian tastes. For instance, $j = 2$ means that you would just be willing to tax man A (or generation A) £4 to be able to give £1 to man B (or generation B) if A is consuming twice as much as B. (If $j = 3$, replace £4 by £8; if $j = 1$, replace £4 by £2.) Any number can play this game. Suppose $j = 2$; then if $a = 0.01$, the best long-run ratio of net investment to net output is $1/7$. If $a = 0.02$, $s^* = 1/8$. If $a = 0.01$ but $j = 3$, $s^* = 1/10$. If $a = 0.01$ but $j = 1$, $s^* = 0.25$. Nobody is very sure about current ratios of net investment to net output, but they are probably quite a bit lower than that.

Another way to look at it may help. I mentioned that the best steady state is characterized by $r^* = a+jf$, where r^* is the best value for the steady-state marginal product of capital. With $a = 0.01$ and $j = 2$, that condition says $r^* = 0.07$. Nobody knows what the net rate of return on capital is in modern industrial economies, but the size of pre-tax rates of profit suggest that it must be quite a lot higher than 7 per cent a year.

Only one more thing needs to be said. I have, as usual, been concentrating on the optimal steady state, and not on the optimal approach to the optimal steady state. As usual, my excuse is that the non-steady-state theory is much hairier than the steady-state theory. In the present instance, there is an additional excuse. Recent work by Mirrlees and Stern suggests that there may be only a slight loss in social welfare from following a well-chosen but simple non-optimal policy instead of the optimal policy. In particular, the policy of choosing the best steady-state saving rate and sticking to it from the beginning comes off fairly well in their calculations, provided the initial situation is not altogether too far from the best steady state.

Now it is time to heed my remark about simple formulas. The more common-sense point is a debunking one. Apart from the possibility of influencing the natural rate of growth, strictly economic policy with relation to economic growth has a limited—though I should still say an important— scope. A good choice of policy depends on some subtle aspects of the economic environment and social preferences. There is very little reason to do something just because the Germans or the Japanese do it, or even because the Americans do it Or even because the English do it.

6

Aspects of Economic Policy

THE subjects of the two preceding chapters—the study of an economy with more than one asset as a possible store of wealth, and the analysis of 'best' paths in such an economy starting from arbitrary initial conditions—are still the source of active research. There is an additional obvious need for someone to synthesize the theory of growth, which takes full employment for granted, with the shorter-run macroeconomics whose main subject is variation of the volume of employment. The need for synthesis covers both the descriptive theory and the theory of policy, and it will undoubtedly lead on to more complicated models with more commodities and more assets.

That development lies in the future. In this last chapter, I want only to take up one or two further applications of the theory of growth to problems of economic policy. In no case will I try to give a complete exposition, but only enough of the flavour to suggest that theory does have something interesting to say about practice.

CRITERIA FOR PUBLIC INVESTMENT

The first problem I have in mind has to do with criteria for public investment, especially with the choice of an interest rate for discounting the benefits of public investments. I shall follow some of the work of Kenneth Arrow.

If private and public investment projects are physically the same, then the problem of public investment policy is exactly the problem that we solved in the previous lecture; an optimizing government need only see to it that the right overall volume investment gets done, no matter who does it.

A different problem arises if we step slightly outside the model and suppose that there are two distinct kinds of capital, private industrial capital financed by private savings and public overhead capital financed by income-tax revenues. The private economy is assumed to save and invest in industrial capital a constant fraction of its real income after tax. The government always balances its budget; it spends its tax revenues on overhead capital. Aggregate output depends in the usual way on the stocks of industrial and overhead capital, and on the volume of employment in efficiency units.

This is a situation in which the government does not have complete control over the allocation of output among its three possible uses—private consumption, private investment, and public investment. At any instant, aggregate output is predetermined by the existing stocks of private and public capital and the available supply of labour. If the government had two policy instruments at its command it could, in the best Tinbergen manner, hit two targets: it could control, say, private investment and public investment. Since total output is given, private consumption would be determined as the residual, and the government would have complete control over the allocation of resources.

Instead the government is assumed to have only one instrument, the rate of income tax. By fixing it, the government determines its own tax revenue and therefore, since its budget must balance, the volume of public investment. But the allocation of the rest of total output between consumption and industrial investment depends only on the private propensity to save (and invest) and is not under government control.

Suppose that the government's goal is the maximization of a welfare integral like the one we studied in chapter 5. It wishes to manoeuvre its one policy instrument so as to achieve the best consumption profile among the ones that it can achieve. There are physically feasible consumption profiles that it can not achieve, because its control of resource allocation is imperfect. All the achievable consumption profiles have a given constant ratio of private consumption to private investment.

If the government did have full control, it would obviously allocate investment so as to keep the marginal product of industrial capital equal to the marginal product of overhead capital at every instant of time; if that were not so, aggregate output could be increased by shifting a bit of investment from the sector with lower marginal product to the sector with higher, and that could only be a good thing. Since the government does not have full control, that may not be the best thing to do; it may pay to allow a discrepancy between marginal products of public and private capital if that is necessary in order to get nearer to the right *total* investment.

It turns out that the best achievable policy for the government tends towards a steady state, and I will discuss only what the economy will look like once it gets into the best achievable steady state. There will be an appropriate rate of interest for discounting consumption flows, and that rate of interest will have the same value that it had in chapter 5, and for the same reasons. I showed there that the correct steady-state rate of interest was equal to $a+jf$, where a is the rate of social time preference, j is the negative of the elasticity of the social marginal utility of consumption per head, and f is the steady-state rate of growth of consumption per head, i.e. the rate of labour-augmenting technical progress.

Now Arrow has a very neat argument to show that in the best achievable steady state, the marginal product of public capital (call it r_2) must be equal to $r^* = a+jf$. That is to say, in the terminal steady state, the government should undertake all public investment projects that earn a return at least equal to r^*. When the government has taxed away the resources necessary for public investment, private investment will be a fraction s of what is left.

Arrow's argument that $r_2 = r^*$ in the best steady state goes like this. First of all, think of the chain of events that happens if a dollar is added to steady-state disposable income in any one year, just for that year. Some of it (a fraction

$1 - s$) will be consumed at once, the rest saved and invested, to earn a rate of return, say r_1, the constant steady-state marginal product of private capital. These earnings add to future disposable income and are partly consumed and partly invested in still more private capital, all of which earns the rate of return r_1. And so on. Private capital will be higher at every later time than it would have been had the initial gift of disposable income not occurred. How much higher? Well, suppose that at some later instant it is higher by an amount x. Then private profits will be higher by r_1x, which gives rise to private savings amounting to sr_1x. So x is growing exponentially at rate sr_1. So income is also higher by an amount growing exponentially at the same rate (because the extra private capital earns the constant rate of return r_1); and so is consumption. Provided that r^* is greater than sr_1, the social value of this addition to the consumption stream will be some finite amount, say z, when it is discounted at r^* and added up. The addition of a dollar to disposable income is therefore equivalent in social value to a single act of immediate consumption of value z.

Now consider a government project costing a dollar and yielding, say, a perpetual income stream of r_2. The social welfare loss to the private sector when the government taxes away a dollar to build the project is z; but at each subsequent moment private disposable income is r_2 dollars higher, so there is a perpetual welfare gain of r_2z. Thus, taking account of all interactions, the public project still yields a rate of return r_2, and it should be undertaken provided, and only provided, that r_2 exceeds r^*, the rate at which consumption flows are discounted. Thus, in the terminal steady state, the marginal product of public capital, the rate at which the net benefits from public investments should be discounted for comparison with current construction costs, is $r^* = a + jf$.

How about the marginal product of private capital? Must it be equal to r^* too? Should the government insist that public investments earn the same return as private? If the economy were perfectly controlled, the answer would clearly be yes, as I have already pointed out. It would never pay to pass up a high-yielding project, public or private, in favour of a low-yielding one, public or private. But in this case of a partially-controlled economy it is not so. The public and private rates of return will generally be different.

The easiest way to see this is to take up a special case. Suppose aggregate output is a Cobb–Douglas function of private capital, public capital, and labour (in efficiency units). Suppose the elasticity of output with respect to private capital is b_1, and with respect to public capital b_2. Then, since the elasticity of output with respect to an input is the ratio of the marginal to the average product of the input, we have two equations:

$$b_1 = r_1 v_1 \text{ and } b_2 = r_2 v_2.$$

In the best achievable steady state, $r_2 = r^*$. In addition, there are two Harrod–Domar conditions, one for each type of capital. If we let t stand for the best steady-state tax rate and s for the ratio of private saving to disposable income, then $s(1-t)$ is the ratio of private investment to total output and t is the ratio of public investment to aggregate output. The Harrod–Domar conditions, guaranteeing that both stocks of capital grow at the natural rate g, are

$$gv_1 = s(1-t) \text{ and } gv_2 = t.$$

We have five equations in the five unknowns v_1, v_2, r_1, r_2, t, so all the characteristics of the best achievable steady state are determined.

From these equations it is easily calculated that

$$r_2/r_1 = r^*/r_1 = s(r^* - gb_2)/gb_1.$$

Thus, in the best steady state, the government ought to use a lower or higher rate of interest than that earned on private capital according as $s(r^* - gb_2)$ is smaller or greater than gb_1. The inequality can go either way for arbitrarily chosen parameter values. The only constraint on the parameters is that $r^* > sr_1$; this has to be imposed to make sure the welfare integral converges. But this inequality is equivalent to $r^* > g(b_1 + b_2)$, which is essentially the condition that had to be imposed in the one-capital optimal growth model of the previous chapter. It is still possible for r_1 to be greater or less than r^*.

To get any further we have to make guesses about parameters, and that is not easy with respect to the relative size of b_1 and b_2. Suppose we take $r^* = 0 \cdot 07$ and $g = 0 \cdot 04$ as in the previous chapter. Then if $b_1 = 0 \cdot 20$ and $b_2 = 0 \cdot 05$, the government should use a lower interest rate than private firms if $s < 2/17$. If $b_1 = 0 \cdot 15$ and $b_2 = 0 \cdot 10$, the government should do so only if $s < 1/11$. In fact, net private saving—in the U.S. at least—probably runs about $7\frac{1}{2}$ per cent of net national product at full employment. According to the formula, the asymptotic discount rate should be 11 per cent or $8\frac{1}{2}$ per cent for private investment, compared to 7 per cent for public. In general, the lower the private saving-rate compared with the 'optimal' saving-rate in a fully-controlled economy, the lower the government interest rate ought to be, compared with the private rate. The point is that the best achievable plan is prepared to put up with some inefficiency —some public investment yielding less than the marginal private investment—because having that low-yielding investment is better than not having any more investment at all. If private investment were 'too high', the situation would be reversed. And if the government has another policy tool— another tax, or the possibility of financing some investment by borrowing—it can do better still; it can control private investment too, and the best steady state will have equal yields on both kinds of capital. Then we are back essentially to the one-capital-good model of last week.

COMBINED FISCAL AND MONETARY POLICY

The second application I want to discuss has to do with the choice of a combined monetary-fiscal policy, when full employment is not guaranteed in some other way and so has to be looked after explicitly. For this purpose, I have to go back to the model of a monetary economy that I analysed in chapter 4.

Boiled down to steady-state conditions, the model consisted of two equations in the unknowns m and v; v is the capital/output ratio and $m = M/pQ$ is the ratio of real money balances to real output. The two equations were

$$m = (1-h)s/(1-s)g - v/(1-s),$$

$$m = m(v, r-i+\theta-g).$$

The first of these equations is the locus of points where the Harrod–Domar condition is satisfied; a higher m goes along with a lower v because more private saving is absorbed in maintaining real balances, leaving less private saving for real capital formation, capable of supporting only a lower capital/output ratio. The second equation is a portfolio-balance equation; it makes the demand for money per unit of output an increasing function of total wealth per unit of output and therefore of the capital/output ratio, and a decreasing function of the yield differential between holdings of real capital and of government debt (i is the nominal rate on government debt, and $\theta-g = \phi$ is the steady-state rate of inflation). For given values of the behaviour parameters s and g and the government policy parameters h, i and θ, these two equations determine the only possible steady state that can result.

To pose the policy problem sharply, I am going to choose a special form of the portfolio-balance equation. Suppose that investors demand a certain 'target' rate of return before they are willing to hold real capital at all, and that they will quickly seize all investment opportunities that offer the target rate of return or anything higher. If the return on real capital is just equal to the target rate, investors will absorb money balances and real capital indifferently. It is natural to define the target rate of return by a required margin over the real return on money balances, $i-(\theta-g)$, but that is a genuine hypothesis about the behaviour of investors. Under this assumption, the portfolio-balance equation degenerates into the requirement that

$$r = i-(\theta-g)+u,$$

where u is the required premium over the return on cash balances.

Given that the return on real capital is a decreasing function of the capital/output ratio, the graph of the portfolio-balance curve is no longer smoothly increasing in the $m-v$ plane. Instead, it coincides with the horizontal axis for v less than the number v^* for which $r(v^*) = i-(\theta-g)+u$, and then rises vertically when $v = v^*$ (Figure 11). That is to say,

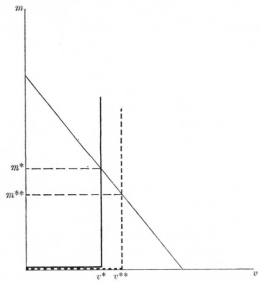

FIG. 11. Determination of steady state with a target rate of return

when v is less than v^* the rate of return on real capital exceeds its target value, investors rush to real capital; they are unwilling to hold government debt at all. When $v = v^*$, investors are indifferent about the composition of their portfolios. When v exceeds v^* the return on real capital provides less than the required premium and investors are prepared to hold indefinite amounts of government debt. Obviously this is an extreme view of investment demand; you can imagine alternative shapes of the portfolio-balance curve that temper this all-or-nothing version but approximate it.

The only possible steady state is the one with $v = v^*$. If v is less than v^* the rate of profit will be 'too high', the investment demand will be essentially unlimited, there will be an inflationary gap. If v exceeds v^* the rate of profit will be too low, investment demand will collapse, there will be unemployment. Given the policy parameters i and θ, the investment demand equation determines the unique capital/output ratio compatible with full employment equilibrium, and does so independently of saving behaviour.

But just having $v = v^*$ does not guarantee full employment. In a steady state with $v = v^*$, the ratio of real net investment to net national product must be gv^* because net investment must be g times the stock of capital. If the government chooses its fiscal-monetary policy arbitrarily, some total of private saving will result, some part of it will be absorbed by the government deficit, and what is left will not necessarily just match the already-determined volume of private investment. The maintenance of full employment in the steady state uses up the degree of freedom provided by the government's fiscal-monetary policy.

It is precisely the generalized Harrod–Domar condition that must be satisfied. It states the condition that private saving should just suffice to absorb the public deficit and provide for the steady-state real investment requirement. Therefore the government's fiscal-monetary policy must generate just so large a public debt that

$$m = M/pQ = \frac{(1-h)s-gv^*}{(1-s)g}$$

If we let δ stand for M'/pY, the ratio of the government's budget deficit to the national product in current prices, we have, since $M' = \theta M$, that the required deficit is

$$\delta = \frac{\theta}{g}\frac{(1-h)s-gv^*}{(1-s)}.$$

In any steady state, the rate of inflation is simply $\theta - g$, so θ is pinned down as soon as the government has a view about the desirable rate of inflation. If, for example, price stability is an object of policy, then θ must be equal to g and the required deficit for full employment becomes

$$\delta = \frac{(1-h)s - gv^*}{(1-s)}$$

Now let us see where we are. The government has three policy instruments at its disposal: θ, the rate of growth of the money supply, i, the nominal interest rate it pays on its debt, and δ, which we can think of as governing the absolute size of the government debt relative to national income. It has, or can have, three policy objectives: full employment, stable prices (or any rate of inflation it prefers), and v^*, the steady-state capital/output ratio that determines just about every other steady-state quantity including consumption per head. If price stability is a goal, we have $\theta = g$ and that uses up one policy instrument. Full employment requires a unique proportional deficit whose relation to v^* we already know. Can the government have a growth policy; can it hope to aim at a chosen asymptotic capital/output ratio and consumption per head; can it, in other words, do the sort of optimization job I have already analysed for a non-monetary centrally-planned economy?

That depends. The rather sharp investment function I have chosen has the virtue of putting the question clearly. There is a required rate of return on real investment, and that required rate of return determines uniquely a capital/output ratio v^*. The only handle the government has on v^* is through the required rate of return; if it can affect one it can affect the other. If the required rate of return is just a fact of nature, there is not much the government can do about it. If, at the other extreme, the required rate of return is simply a premium—a risk premium or normal rate of profit—over and above the real rate of interest on government debt, then the government can have a policy about v^*.

Suppose, as I suggested earlier, that $r = i - (\theta - g) + u$. Then if $\theta = g$ for price stability, $r = i + u$. If the government can choose any non-negative rate of interest, it can then manœuvre r through the range of values exceeding the premium u. That provides a choice among values of v corresponding to that range of values of r; it may be a wide or narrow choice, depending on how the realized rate of profit is related to the capital/output ratio and how wide a range of capital/output ratios the technology permits. If the government would like to achieve a v^* corresponding to a rate of profit less than u, it can do so only by less conventional means. By increasing θ beyond g it can generate a positive rate of inflation and drive the real return on money balances below zero. Or else it can find some way to subsidize investment directly; but then there may be adverse distributional consequences to be taken into account.

To the extent that policy can reduce or increase the required rate of return, the vertical portion of the portfolio-balance curve moves to the right or to the left along the horizontal axis. A lower rate of interest, for example, reduces r and increases v^*. Correspondingly the required m or δ falls along the Harrod–Domar locus. This is the conventional result: The combination of an easy credit policy (low i) and tight budgetary policy (low δ) is capable in principle of maintaining full employment while shifting the output-mix in favour of investment. The lower interest rate induces private investors to hold more real capital, and the reduced deficit allows the extra capital to displace government debt in the balance sheets of private savers.

I said 'capable in principle' because it is notoriously difficult to isolate in real data the influence of monetary and credit conditions on investment in fixed capital. But the case is not really clear. It is one thing to claim that investment decisions are rather insensitive to credit conditions in the short run because other, more sensational, things are happening simultaneously; and it is something else to believe that even in long run steady-state full-employment conditions, asset preferences are insensitive to relative yields. Even if we accept the optimistic view of monetary policy for the long run, there is a further pessimistic factor to be thrown into the balance. I have been assuming, in effect, that the government's interest-bearing debt is legal tender; the Treasury simply covers its deficit by issuing bonds at par bearing whatever coupon rate it chooses. In the more realistic case that the Treasury has to sell its bonds, it would not be possible to squeeze bondholders permanently by letting the price-level rise. The nominal interest rate would presumably rise by the steady rate of inflation. But there would still be some scope for debt-management policy.

STEADY-STATE CONSUMPTION AND THE
SAVING RATE

It may be worth while to mention one other elementary application of the steady-state relations in the model. For this purpose I revert to the non-monetary model with a Cobb–Douglas production function. In the Cobb–Douglas case, it is easily calculated that $q = Av^{b/1-b}$ where q is output per efficiency unit of labour and A is a constant that plays no role. In a steady state, the Harrod–Domar relation $s = gv$ tells us that $q = Bs^{b/1-b}$ where B is another constant. From this it is obvious that the elasticity of steady-state output per head (in efficiency units) with respect to the steady-state saving rate is $b/1-b$ or about $1/3$ if $b = 1/4$, more or less. In other words, a 1 per cent (not 1 percentage point) increase in the saving rate will, if full employment is maintained, eventually lead to a new steady state in which output per head is $1/3$ of 1 per cent higher.

Consumption per head is $(1-s)q$. Since the elasticity of a product is the sum of the elasticities, the elasticity of consumption per head with respect to the steady-state saving rate is $b/(1-b)-s/(1-s)$. That is lower than the output-elasticity, because the higher saving-rate reduces the ratio of consumption to output. For $b = 0.25$ and $s = 0.075$, this elasticity works out to about one-quarter. Thus an increase in the saving rate to, say, 0.09, which is a 20 per cent increase, will lead to an initial reduction in consumption per head, because more is being saved out of an almost unchanged output, and eventually to a level of consumption per head in efficiency units 5 per cent higher in perpetuity than with the lower saving-rate. The theory of optimal saving that I expounded in chapter 5 is a systematic way of deciding whether this kind of shift is worth while. This calculation also confirms a proposition that I stated very near the beginning: consumption per head is maximized among steady states when its elasticity with respect to s is zero, that is, when $s/(1-s) = b/(1-b)$, or when $s = b$, or, using the Harrod–Domar condition, when $g = b/v = r$.

Conclusion

I AM inclined to think that not much more than this can be extracted from the one-sector theory of growth. That is not to say that I would be very surprised to pick up the next issue of a learned journal and discover that someone has found a new way to use the model or has managed to incorporate in it more general assumptions about technology or time preference or something else. In fact, more general assumptions than any I have described can already be handled, although not very transparently. That is a useful activity, but I am not now thinking of publishable results but of usable insights into real economies.

I am trying to express an attitude towards the building of very simple models. I don't think that models like this lead directly to prescription for policy or even to detailed diagnosis. But neither are they a game. They are more like reconnaissance exercises. If you want to know what it's like out there, it's all right to send two or three fellows in sneakers to find out the lay of the land and whether it will support human life. If it turns out to be worth settling, then that requires an altogether bigger operation. The job of building usable larger-scale econometric models on the basis of whatever analytical insights come from simple models is much more difficult and less glamorous. But it may be what God made graduate students for. Presumably he had something in mind.

Bibliography

Chapter 1

As mentioned in the text, cross-country data can be found in *Why Growth Rates Differ* by Edward F. Denison (Brookings Institution, 1967). These cover only a relatively short period. A longer run of data for the United States is analysed in 'Factor Prices, Productivity and Growth,' by J. Kendrick and R. Sato (*American Economic Review*, December, 1963). The U.S. Bureau of the Census published in 1966 a useful compendium of data in *Long-term Economic Growth 1860–1965*.

The origin of the Harrod–Domar condition is in Harrod's *Towards a Dynamic Economics* (Macmillan, 1948, Lecture Three) and Domar's 'Capital Expansion, Rate of Growth and Employment' (*Econometrica*, April, 1946). The variation of the saving rate through changes in the distribution of income is used in Nicholas Kaldor's 'Alternative Theories of Distribution,' (*Review of Economic Studies*, Vol. XXIII, No. 2, 1955–6) as the key to the satisfaction of the Harrod–Domar condition.

Chapter 2

There is a voluminous literature on the introduction of a variable capital-output ratio. It is summarized in F. H. Hahn's and R. C. O. Matthews' monumental survey article 'The Theory of Economic Growth' (*Economic Journal*, December, 1964) which covers some of the same ground as this book and contains an extensive bibliography. An excellent textbook treatment at a more advanced level is E. Burmeister's and A. R. Dobell's *Mathematical Theories of Economic Growth* (Macmillan, 1970); this book contains ample references to the more recent literature.

For an example of an endogenous theory of the 'bias' of technological progress, see P. A. Samuelson: 'A Theory of Induced Innovation along Kennedy–Weizsäcker lines' (*Review of Economics and Statistics*, November, 1965). The relation between the steady-state rate of interest and the speed of technical progress is studied in 'The Relation between the Rate of Interest and the Rate of Technical Progress' by D. Levhari and E. Sheshinski (*Review of Economic Studies*, July, 1969).

Chapter 3

The model in this chapter is necessarily difficult. The original source is 'Neoclassical Growth with Fixed Factor Proportions' by R. Solow, J. Tobin, C. C. von Weizsäcker and M. Yaari (*Review of Economic Studies*, April, 1966). It has been carried further by D. Cass and J. Stiglitz in 'The Implications of Alternative Savings and Expectations Hypotheses for Choices of Technique and Patterns of Growth' (*Journal of Political Economy*, July/August, 1969, Part II).

Chapter 4

The basic reference is J. Tobin: 'Money and Economic Growth' (*Econometrica*, October, 1965). See also M. Sidrauski: 'Inflation and Economic Growth' (*Journal of Political Economy*, December, 1967). There are several related articles in the May, 1969, issue of the *Journal of Money, Credit and Banking*. For the important analogy to the case of many capital goods, see F. Hahn: 'Equilibrium Dynamics with Heterogeneous Capital Goods' (*Quarterly Journal of Economics*, November, 1966) and K. Shell and J. Stiglitz: 'The Allocation of Investment in a Dynamic Economy' (*Quarterly Journal of Economics*, November, 1967).

Chapter 5

The source is F. Ramsey's 'A Mathematical Theory of Saving' (*Economics Journal*, December, 1928). More recent treatments are D. Cass: 'Optimum Growth in an Aggregative Model of Capital Accumulation' (*Review of Economic Studies*, July, 1965) and *Essays on the Theory of Optimal Economic Growth*, edited by K. Shell (M.I.T. Press, 1967) which contains a bibliography. A somewhat unorthodox treatment is to be found in M. Inagaki's forthcoming book on *Optimal Economic Growth* (North–Holland, 1970). There is an interesting forthcoming paper on approximate optimality by J. Mirrlees and N. Stern: 'On Fairly Good Plans.'

Chapter 6

K. Arrow's work on discounting is to be found in 'Discounting and Public Investment Criteria' (in A. V. Kneese and S. C. Smith, eds.: *Water Research*, Johns Hopkins University Press, 1966). For the management of a growing economy, see the article by Tobin already cited; also P. Diamond's 'National Debt in a Neoclassical Growth Model' (*American Economic Review*,

December, 1965) and 'Optimal Fiscal and Monetary Policy and Economic Growth' by D. Foley, K. Shell, and M. Sidrauski (*Journal of Political Economy*, July/August, 1969).

An excellent collection of republished articles is *Readings in the Theory of Economic Growth* (M.I.T. Press, 1970) edited by J. Stiglitz and H. Uzawa. A similar series of readings edited by A. K. Sen is to appear in the *Penguin Modern Economics* series.